Poems Are My Love

Myles W. Wallace

Order this book online at www.trafford.com
or email orders@trafford.com

Most Trafford titles are also available at major online book retailers.

ISBN: 978-1-4907-2932-9 (sc)
ISBN: 978-1-4907-2933-6 (e)

Trafford rev. 02/27/2014

 www.trafford.com

North America & international
toll-free: 1 888 232 4444 (USA & Canada)
fax: 812 355 4082

Thank God!

This book is dedicated in Memory of My Mother, Jennie,
My Father, Melvin, and My Brothers, James and David

26 Letters

From A to Z
They describe everything
Some untold
Too few unseen

Try and name something
Without using them
You will see
They always win

26 letters
Started the beginning
26 letters
Will finish the ending

Around world they are used
With the English Language
You even need them
For universal changes

Top to bottom
Or inside out
No matter what you do
They have the clout

26 letters are always there
When you need them
They were made
Just to please you

30 Second Lover

Wham Bam Thank you Ma'am!
That is my bag
I don't have time to make love
To me it's a drag

I am not your man
If you want an all night thing
In less than a minute
I'll be ready for another fling

I'm a 30 second lover
I don't like to hang around
I'm a 30 second lover
I don't have time to get down

If you want to be fondled and caressed
You have got to get someone else
If you like to hug and kiss
I won't have anything left

If you want to be wined and dined
Don't even bother to ask
If you like to dance and be romanced
On my agenda that's passed

I'm a 30 second lover
Don't say you want to get hooked
I'm a 30 second lover
Bye! My half-minute is up

A Spark Of Your Love

A spark of your love
Is like thunder from above
A spark of your love
Puts lightning in my heart
One flick of your bic
Like pow!—It does the trick

You turn me on and
I can't turn me off
Like a doorknob
I feel boss

A spark of your love
Is dose from above
Lightning, thunder, fire
All in one

You are lightning without pain
Thunder without rain and
Fire without smoke

A spark of your love
Inspired me to write this song

A Special Kind Of Love

This is love in unique form
True to life
Love adorned

Not between man and wife
Man and child
Though not that simplified

Aged and mild
A love that cannot be denied

Affection tender and deep
Blossomed and blooming
Love that will forever keep

Dedicated to forever—renewing
Perpetuating throughout the world
Adolescence to adulthood

A love between man and girl
Father and daughter
Acquiring womanhood

A Thousand Reasons To Separate

Division started on the way from Africa
Call it colonial influenced dissension
The inability to cooperate
Began at the start of our adverse adventure

We can blame it on the captors
Or the delayed start of self-autonomy
Disunity remains today
A web of disharmony

We separate because of melanin
Black, brown, fair

We fragment because of education
College, High School, Elementary

We separate because of income
White collar, blue collar, welfare

We separate because of residence
Uptown, downtown, almost there

We find a thousand reasons to separate
None of them are logical
With a thousand reasons to separate
Compromise seems improbable

Our ancestors fought valiantly
To keep our integrity intact
400 years later
We disregard their acts

Voting rights
Gave us establishment flavor
When the election arrives
That day we do not savor

We separate because of politics
Democrat, Republican, Independent

We separate for religion
Catholic, Protestant, Baptist

We separate for status
High-class, middle-class, average-class

We separate because of style
Clubs, lounges, don't go anywhere

We separate because of dress
Tuxedos, suits, leisure

We separate because of automobiles
Mercedes, Cadillac, Beater

We have a thousand reasons to separate
None of them are valid
With a thousand reasons to separate
We will never be together

After Living In The Past, I Presently Want You To Be My Future

I constantly thought of how things used to be
Yes, how I once was in love
I would even dream about other affairs
I had feelings for no one

You see, my love left,
She just went away and
My world fell apart
Now that I have met you
You will remain in my heart

After living in the past,
I presently want you to be my future
After living in the past
I presently want you to be my future

I could not think of anything but
How I had been hurt so bad
You made me forget all of that
To be with you, I am so glad

To you. I owe a world of happiness
I always want you near
No one will ever take your place and
There are no more tears

After living in the past
I presently want you to be my future
After living in the past
No other I have use for

As Rhyme Three Times

An image of you and me
Cruised through mind . . . .

Candlelight and wine
With you beside

The night flowed like pollen
In a breeze
Honey-sugar, indeed

I hugged you oh so tight
As we danced into the night
Your beauty—so bright

You tasted like candy
Just plain sweet

Of each other we are a part
You are my heart
You are the ace of my cards

Bakerman

Busting out all over
His stomach hid his waist
When he laughed
His belly spilled
All over the place

If he relaxed
His tummy would expand
He couldn't push it back
Even with both hands

Bakerman wasn't a pudgy fellow
Bakerman's life was just mellow

If he stood up
It would slightly disappear
Looking at the matter
It became all too clear

He didn't eat much
It just stayed in his gait
Then became a part of his pants
And remained that way

Bakerman the sugar fan
Bakerman had a sweet plan

Myles W. Wallace

Battlefield Promotion

Woman you have stood by me
Through thick and thin
You have fought with me
When I thought I could never win

From everyday confrontations
To all out warfare
I could depend on you
To always be there

I am going to give you
A battlefield promotion
General of the family
You are a five star wonder
For life that you handle

You do not use weapons
Just your clever charm
Any volatile situation
You can disarm

You never use threats
Or deceptive tactics
Your philosophy is to act
Not to start attacking

You will not use propaganda
You just say what you feel and
No matter how explosive the setting
You can always strike a deal

You deserve a battlefield promotion
A Medal of Honor
That is only the beginning
For your love, dedication, devotion

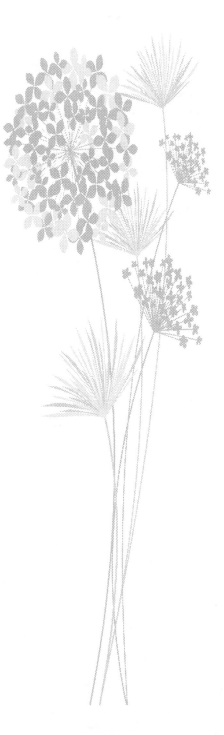

Beautiful In Your Own Beautiful Way

Yes, you're beautiful
You're beautiful as a sunny summer day

You are prettier than the day is long
Stunning attraction all your own

From head to toe you are my only dream
Totally gorgeous that is what I mean

The sight, touch and taste of you
Ooh baby, you're just too cool!

Your hair is like silken thread
Soft and cuddly all over your head

Lips so moist, they feel so nice
Kissing you brings me to life

Your face could light the darkened night
Seeing you is pure delight

Your hands should possess a magic wand
And I want to be your only one

Your legs just make me gleam
Yeah baby, you are venus in blue jeans

You are a part of me, just like a bite
And I must say you are more beautiful than life

You are beautiful, beauty divine
Oh I how wish, you were all mine

Better Safe, Than Sorry

See the hitchhiker
Thumbing a ride
Press the gas
Pass him by

Look at the people
Peddling wares
Keep your money
Don't take a chance

Better safe, than sorry
It's better to say
There he goes, instead of
There he lays

If you see a person
Blocking your path
Stop and look
For another path

If you want to party
At some far out place
Take a rain check
To save face

Better safe, than sorry
Is the only way
Better safe, than sorry
Is the best fate

Big Wally

Oh! He's big!
Built like a tree
Must of stood
Near seven feet

When he spoke
It was more a roar
People shook
They thought he controlled

Big Wally
Took no jive
Big Wally
Was a high five

He had an education
A carpenter by trade
In his spare time
With children he played

He was friendly as a kitten
With a reputation that
He shrugged off
As misrepresentation

Big Wally was
Gentle
Big Wally
Sentimental

Bingo

Is it good baby
Am I doing you right
Are my motions fluid
Do I have it tight

Do we move in unison to
Touch every sensitive spot
Have I the staying power
To be on top

She'll just smile and say
Bingo!
I knew I was home free

Then she would laugh and shout
Bingo!
She was fantastic company

For her heart
I was an arrow straight
To capture her mind
With no escape

The times we are together
Love we possess
I never want to part
We have complete happiness

When I look into her eyes
Her lips pout
Bingo!

We are both winners
With our count
Bingo!

Blowout!

I was sitting in my pad
Listening to my box
Just cooling out
But I couldn't quite hear it
I figured it wasn't loud enough

I was playing my favorite song
Of all time
Burn, baby, burn
Nibbling on some nuggets and
Tasting some cherry wine

I had four huge speakers
And four sub-woofers

Each speaker consisted of
A crossover network
A twenty-inch bass hoofer

A pair of horns
Four high-range tweeters and
Six mid-range hookers

They were driven by
Eight high-power amps
I could reproduce a sonic boom
In my soundproof room

I got up off the couch and went
To check out my box
I was looking for the volume knob
To turn up my throbbing sound

I dialed it a quarter
It still wasn't loud
I started thinking
My ears must be plugged

I knew each speaker could put out 250 watts
The amplifiers were good for 500
The system was together and
I was feeling mellow

I revolved the knob another eighth
I didn't hear a sound
I spun it to half
There was shaking of the ground

A blowout was coming!
A blowout was coming!

I cranked the volume knob
Three more notches
But it still wasn't loud
I thought
Is my mind on a cloud

The furniture began to move
Pictures were coming down
The walls started vibrating and
I couldn't hear one little sound

Blowout was near!
Blowout was clear!

Just before I swung the knob
For all of its play
I stopped at nine-tenths way

My windows began to rattle
The door commenced to sway
But for all the action
Music didn't come my way

To hear my favorite song
I finally reached my limit
I twisted the knob
To the maximum limit

By this time the music was so loud
The dog started to grimace
But I didn't hear anything
My pet was my witness

Ten seconds later
The house flew apart
The roof went first
Landing in my neighbors back yard

The finale followed
When my speakers blasted aside
Pieces went every kind of way
But I never heard a sound

I finally discovered
Why music never came my way
I had my head-phones on
Unplugged of course
Something I didn't find out
Until later that day

Full power baby
That is what I observed
I know what they mean
When they say
Action speaks louder than words!

Blowout the final phase!
Blowout all the way!

Boyfriend

Your boyfriend gets in our way
Why don't you get rid of him
He stops us from being together
I want to come over and play

When I call you
The conversation is always too short
With him on the extension
I hardly hear your voice

Every time I plan a date
Something always goes wrong
I know it's that dude
Who listens on the phone

Your boyfriend gets in our way
He is stopping us from being happy
The guy has become a nuisance
Preventing our love from lasting

I remember the time I picked you up
To go to the Bulls' game
You kept looking out of the window
To see if he wanted the same

I know he is the type that
Shoots first and later cries
It doesn't matter to me
You are the gleam in my eyes

Your boyfriend gets in my way
Tell him to hit the road Jack
And also tell him, I said
To never look back

Brainwashed

I thought I had a good woman
She left me—gone
She didn't say a word
Took all of my funds

She had me fooled
With the game she played
I a content man
Now full of heartache

I have been brainwashed
Worse than Frankenstein
I have been brainwashed
Man she was fine

She led me on
Like a thirst-stricken man to water
I took her love for real
I had more than I ought to

She caught me in her web
I gave anything she wanted
She knew exactly what to do
As I stumbled and faltered

I was brainwashed
Just like a P.O.W.
I have been brainwashed
A total lobotomy

Bull

The young bull
Races down the hill
Leaps over a fence
To get one female

Bull saunters to the ring
No need to hurry
He is in control
Because he is king

Anyone he chooses
Will become his mate
His determination provides
No escape

Bull never raises his voice
Or uses his horns
He doesn't throw his weight around
Nor stamp the ground

Bull.

If bull loses his temper
He charges straight ahead
Explosions pepper all
All that are far
Those that are near

Bull is the master
He has no ritual
He conquers everyone
With no residuals

Bull has a coat of armor
A will of steel
His confidence is impenetrable
With blazing speed

Bull.

Bullet

It rips and tears
Shatters and disfigures
Shreds-maims
By pulling a trigger

A ball of lead
Which costs less than a penny
Can put a human being in
The state of eternity

Bullet has no conscious
For whom it destroys
Discharged in an aimless direction
Treated like a toy

Bullet buy it by the dozen
Bullet don't even sort it

It flashes out of a barrel at
Many miles per second
It screams as it
Flies for an intended target

Its trajectory is irreversible
Direction is nondescript
There is no remorse
Smashing its victim

Bullet memories it doesn't retain
Bullet hurting with no refrain

Myles W. Wallace

Bullseye (Right On Target)

I was making love with my baby
When she said: "I wasn't hitting it right"
I thought I was really getting down
We had been doing it all night

No matter what I did or
How hardy I did it
To her I wasn't potent enough
Long and hard I was stroking
She told me she wanted
The "real hot stuff"

We abruptly switched positions
She had been on top
With my new state of heart
I began to show her
What a kind of man I was about

I maneuvered to the left
I glided it to the right
I probed deeper and deeper
I grazed her pearl real nice

My rhythm got faster
As we went up and down
She yelled, baby you've hit bullseye
(Right on target)

Her eyes became glassy
When she began to shout
Oh baby, you scored a bullseye
(Right on target)

Her thrashing and twisting
Changed to silky, smooth passion
Her delicious lips pantomimed
Absolute satisfaction

We grooved together
Spontaneously climaxing
Ecstasy propelled us
With rapid reaction

My baby, spoke softly, and said:
"Daddy, you hit bullseye"
(Right on target)

Whispering, she was barely audible
She repeated: "Sweetie, you hit bullseye"
(Right-on target)

I observed her angel face
Then kissed her parted mouth
I knew she could not deny
I hit bullseye (right on target)

Equipped with victory
I was prepared to indulge again
She moved next to me and grinned

She said: "Darling no more please
You've hit bullseye
At least twenty-five times"
(Right on target)

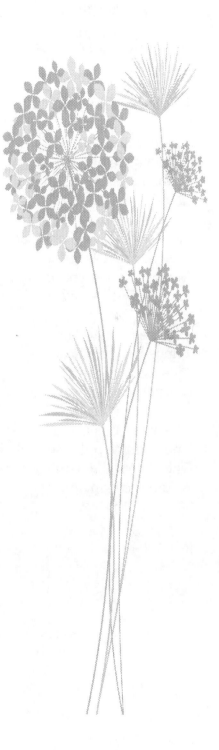

Bumblebees In The Line (Busy Signal)

From everywhere I call my girl
I hear a buzzing sound
Is the circuit operating properly
Or shorted to ground

It doesn't matter what time it is
Morning, noon or night
I can't get through
Not once, but twice

The bumblebees in the line
Shield my girl
Bumblebees in the line
Guard her world

Are they making honey or
Just having a little fun
Maybe it is a meeting of the minds
Or a time for relaxation

I will keep on trying
I hope she hangs up
I just want to talk to
My sweet rosebud

There are bumblebees in the line
I have got to get them out
There are bumblebees in the line
And remove my doubt

Candy Cane

She's not like a licorice stick
Or a lollipop
She is a sweet young thing
Her name is candy cane

Not like a gingersnap
Or a chocolate chip
Go with her and you'll find
She's quite a trip

Cap'n

He took control
Ran a tight ship
Just like America
He ruled with an iron fist

There were no midnight runs
On his vessel they just weren't made
If someone got caught
The plank became his aid

Cap'n-no, not Hook
Cap'n-Ahab he wasn't

Any mutineer
Would be met by Bligh
He would pull yeoman's duty
To hoist the frigate's flag high

Then a kangaroo court
Would hold trial
Cap'n would never stand by and
See his craft go down

Cap'n-not Video time
Cap'n-Kirk style

Casey (Roll Over) Baseball Strike

America's past time today—1981
Stopped with long term negotiations
All parties are losing
Struck with ramifications

Take me out to the ballpark
Exists no more
While veiled boards
Reveal no score

Apart at the seams
Has come the game
For playing outdoors

Casey (roll over)
Oh! What a shame
Baseball strike

Casey (move over)
Delayed entry into
The hall of names
The baseball strike

The first strike in baseball history
Occurred in mid-season
It rejected millions of fans
Without rhyme or reason

There will be no stars
Come the break
No one can stand
To earn his pay

Free swinging men
Are ready to go to work
The union says
Compensation first

Summer without baseball
Pending compromise
Children are left without heroes
Surely, these are troubled times

Casey (turn over)
You lived once without
A baseball strike

Casey (slide over)
Make room for the owners
With this baseball strike

Do not forget the umpires
Shouting, pointing fingers
No one they can dictate to now
And they are getting kind of squeamish

Stadiums are deserted
Silent star spangled banners
Grass is growing
Gone are the vendors

Casey (roll over)
For the baseball strike
Where is Sister Kay?
Her head hangs for this disgrace

Casey (roll over)
Baseball strike
No music today
For this abandoned game

The baseball strike

Chocolate Sundae

This lady does not walk
Into your life she flows
Just like her namesake—Miss Universe
She is the star of the show

She has got personality plus
Man, she dresses fine
Nothing is to good for this lady
The best that money can buy

Uptown is where
She sparkles in style
At the height of her career
She is a woman of many smiles

At home
She is a lady of design
Taurus verifies her motto
Which characterizes her mind

Chocolate Sundae
She is as smooth as can be
Chocolate Sundae
Sugar coated candy

When we are together
My nights melt into day
She is so sensitive
Any hurt just drifts away

Her eyes are dark and mystic
They accent her delicate touch
She has got dynamic humor
Being near her is a must

She is a leader of happiness
And a giver of care
With her distinctive style
Love fills the air

Black on black in black
She is a exquisite lover
When I sample her hot kisses
I melt just like butter

Chocolate Sundae
My heart she has won
Chocolate Sundae is
My fountain of love

Class

It is not way you talk
But how you move your lips
It is not the way you walk
But how you sway your hips

It is the pleasing smile you have
That makes me do flips
It is how your eyes sparkle
That makes you so hep

Baby, you have class
You belong at the front of the line
Baby, you have class
Take your own sweet time

When we go out
You know exactly what to do
I don't have to say anything
You stay in the groove

Your position in life
Will always be the top
In my heart
You occupy the number one slot

Darling, you have class
In all ways you are right
Sweetheart, you have class
Your love is out-of-sight

Clever

He is a real hep dude
Who has been around
No one knows
This man about town

He is deceptively shy
Never has much to say
When the ladies talk
He looks the other way

Clever misses a wink
Clever catches with a blink

He dresses in
The 1990's style
His feet stand
On solid ground

His automobile is
The classy kind
His condominium
Just off lake shore drive

Clever is top of the line
Clever is right on time

Confessions

On the sofa we sit
My girl and me
I pull her close
To say something sweet

I tell her
Baby you are special to me
I love you sure

I observed you grow
From girl to woman
I view you mature

Confessions are special thoughts
Confessions are admired results

I always want to kiss you
You I love to caress
My joy was true in the past

As it is now
I am elated that
We are passionately involved

Confessions are secret feelings
Confessions are a heart revealing

Conflict

It's when you love someone and
Don't let it show
Because you don't want
That certain person to know

It's when you feel something
And can't let it flow
Because you're afraid
To let yourself go

Conflict is internal confusion
Conflict is external delusion

You want to call that special person
But the phone you can't dial
You long for a hello
So that you can smile

You want to ask that unique person
To go out on a date
But you stay in your shelter
You say it's too late

Conflict is uncertain decision
Conflict is interior division

Crime (Colors)

White crime
Red for crime
Green in crime
Black on black crime

Blue to crime
Brown with crime
Purple follows crime
Yellow after crime

Crime involves all colors
And weapons don't distinguish
Criminals could care less
If you are a victim

Crime steals your pride
Robs your integrity
Betrays your virtue
Deceives your sincerity

Crime is a rainbow
A myriad of questions
A swarm of uncertainty
A whirlpool of solutions

Crisis

It happens everyday
Circumstances out of the norm
It is the substance of
Murphy's Law

Like not having enough money
As hard as you work
Or getting caught in traffic
That frazzles your nerves

You don't have the right clothes
When you go out to party
So you stand in a corner
While everyone dances hearty

Crisis is a personal situation
Crisis has confined ramifications

It's when you like to dine, but
You can't afford the prices and
Those downtown advertisements
Are so very enticing

The vacation you have dreamed
You have to put it off and
If the predicament becomes any worse
From your job you walk

Crisis, hard luck dissension
Crisis, traumatic intervention

Curls For The Girls, Butter For The Brothers

I want all you children
To gather round
I am going to show you
How to paint the town

Been using oil and creams
To keep your head together
Throw it all away
Because I've got something
A whole lot better

It's not lay them straight
Or conk-a-ling
Not dixie peach
Or duke and things

It's called curls for the girls
Butter for the brothers
Here me good, no kidding
It's called curls for you girls
Butter you brothers

It won't take whole lot
There's no muss
A little dab will do you
Never again will you fuss

Pitch those hot combs
Tear off those stocking caps
You won't need a plastic bag
Or a fish net
For the perm you will get

Toss the blow dryer
Yank it from the socket
A pick you won't need
Then watch those waves rocket

Jeri never looked better
Because I've got the good stuff
Do rags are done
Rollers are obsolete
And it won't cost you that much

It's called curls for the girls
Butter my brothers
Let me say it again
It's called curls you girls
Butter on brothers

Days

Monday is blue
Tuesday is yellow
Wednesday is red
Thursday is orange
Friday is green
Saturday is black
Sunday is white

Debt: A Fact Of Life

Are the best things in life free
When prices are soaring
Inflation rampant
And work is at a shortage

When I go to the supermarket
To size up a loaf of bread
It is out of my price range
I settle for nothing instead

Forget about a car
I cannot think about a house
Entertainment is a fantasy
I will have to live without

Debt: A fact of life
Buyer beware
Debt: A fact of life
You better think twice

Education has a premium cost
It is better to cruise the mall
Walking is healthy
Cheaper than gasohol

Living has become expensive
It is more than just survival
To not succeed at living
Is a form of self-denial

Debt: A fact of life
There is no fun in this game
Debt: A fact of life
They are one in the same

Desperate Men With Desperate Motives

They rob and steal
These outlaws will do anything for a dollar
Looking for work
Never entered their minds
Like it ought to

They are desperate men with desperate motives
You can call them desperadoes
They are desperate men with desperate motives
Totally abominable

They come in all sizes, shapes and forms
You can identify them
From the shadows in which they lurk
They always try to two-time you
For sure they are jerks

Perhaps their behavior is caused by
An expensive girlfriend
Maybe it is an exhausted bank account
Because of their despicable ways
People are left without

There is supposed to be good in everyone
For these individuals it remains to be seen
Everyone loses when they are fleeced
By criminals disgraceful schemes

Desperate men with desperate motives
Just call them hoodlums
These desperate men with desperate motives will
Rob you blind
From kit to caboodle

Did You Ever Love Me

Did you ever love me
Did you even care
I can't believe
All in love is fair

Didn't you love me just a little
We were together one year
I know you liked me
You said have no fear

Did you ever love me
Just for one second
Can you ever love me
To breakup never

Please give me an answer
Your emotions I never questioned
I want to touch your tenderness
For your sweetness I am thirsty

My thoughts of you are constant
You are my heart
Of my life
You have become a part

Will you ever love me
As earth beats time
Would you ever love me
To share our minds

Dike: (The Ft. Wayne Story)

A.D. 1982
Forty days and forty nights
Of rain were repeated
Then water over banks
Slowly receded

Residents had piled sandbags high
To beat the river's crest
The flood stage was leveled
They had done their best

Dike: The Ft. Wayne Story
Mission accomplished—no finger
Dike: The Ft. Wayne Story
Civilians became leaders

Property damage was estimated in
The millions of dollars
Rescuers saved several lives
Citizens never stopped erecting the levy
Which broke the tide

Mothers, fathers, sisters and brothers
Bonds became strong
A city of humankind
Now stands as solid wall

Dike: The Ft. Wayne Story is
A Gibraltar rock
Dike: The Ft. Wayne Story has
With no fault

Do Not Disturb

Knock, knock, knock

"Can't you read
I am with my baby
Making love
I am not going to leave"

Knock, Knock, Knock

"She is mine
I won't give her up
I don't care if
Check-out is one o'clock"

Knock! Knock! KnocK!

"I've paid my rent
Just go away
Leave me be
So that I can play!"

KNOCK! KNOCK! KNOCK!

"I've been working
I need some rest
Eight straight hours
I gave my best"

KNOCK! KNOCK! KNOCK!

"Open the door
You locked me out
I am the one that
You are talking about!"

Drum Stix—Page 1

I don't want no chicken
I just want to be lickin' with
My drum stix, drum stix
A rat a tat tat
A rat a tat tat

I don't want no bird
I just want to be heard
With my drum stix, drum stix
A boom, a boom, a boom
Boom, boom, boom

I don't want no turkey, turkey!
I just want to play flirty
With my drum stix, drum stix
A cymbal, cymbal, cymbal
Cymbal, cymbal, cymbal

I don't want no duck
I just want to go
Cluck, cluck, cluck
With my drum stix, drum stix

I want to play my drums
To the wee hours of night
I want to play my drums
And bring up the light

I want to beat my drums
And put on a show
I want to play my drums
Till I can't play no more

(Play drums)

The rooster won't be pickin'
Because I'll just be a flickin'
With my drum stix, drum stix
A knock, knock, knock
A knock, knock, knock

The hen won't be layin'
Cause I'll just be a playin'
My drum stix, drum stix
A tic, tic, tic
Tic, tic, tic

Drum Stix

The goose won't be hoofin'
Cause I'll be doing the cookin'
A knack, a knack, a knack
Knack, knack, knack

The yard will be stompin'
Cause we're all gonna be jumpin
To my drum stix, drum stix

A boom, a boom, a boom
A clack, a clack, clack
Tic, tic, tic

Drum solo: (Your Notes)

Drum roll

(Improvise)

Dying On The Vine

Like a mellon
Without any sun
Our torrid romance
Has lost its heart

The sweetness we had
Has turned bitter
Inside our haven
If I could just remember

Our love is dying on the vine
Rapidly it withered
Love is dying on the vine
Worse than any desert

The light of our lives
Is covered with clouds
The only water produced
Comes from my eyes

Our foundation stands
On parched land
The roots of our love reach out
For survival they grasp

Our love is dying on the vine
Compassion it is without
Love is dying on the vine
Our emotions have dried out

E.R.A. Woman

For a good man
Home you will stay
You have fortitude
Enough to have a baby

Your right to vote
Too long illusive
Your right for equality
Remains inconclusive

E.R.A. Woman
Hang tuff, hang tight
E.R.A. Woman
Win this fight

Insensitive legislators
Out of touch with time
They forgot their mothers
In whom they confide

They think their spouses
Are a piece of furniture
To be used and
Eventually be discarded

E.R.A. Woman
You are a winner
E.R.A. Woman
The beginning

Elevator Love

I met her on her way up
I was feeling so down
She uplifted my spirits
Love I thought I had found

But with her, I don't know
When I am on top
Or headed toward the bottom
To go even lower

Elevator love is
Like a rollercoaster
With elevator love
My feelings
Are out from under

I am happy one day
Sad the next
It is like riding a wave
My emotions are mixed

Like being propelled
Through space
Prepared for a landing
I am ready to touchdown
Without proper planning

Elevator love
Makes me feel capsized
Elevator love is
A bout with time

Encore

I've wined and dined you at
The finest places around town
I took you partying
So we could really get down

In chauffeured carriages
We've seen the sights
We watched the moon
Brighten nights

What do I do for an encore
I've done everything I could
What do I do for an encore
All things under the sun

We've made love
Twelve continuous hours
Then I woke you
To champagne and flowers

Kisses and candy
Are the order of the day
Trinkets of appreciation always
Come your way

What can I do for an encore
I'm not certain
What will I do for an encore
I will keep on searching

Equal Justice For All

They both hold positions
Doing the same job
But in just six short months
For a promotion
One is rejected
While the other is elevated
To be his chief executive

One resides in the suburbs
With a limousine and chauffeur
The other stays in a housing complex
Trying not to become broker

One gulps champagne
The other sips beer
One has the world at his fingertips
The other can't see tomorrow clear

Equal justice for all
That is what the constitution said
Equal justice for all
Discrimination is law of this land

They both see hard times and
One steals a loaf of bread
Just to survive
While the other embezzles millions
Because he wants to live much higher

They both go to prison
One for the rest of his life
The other lives at a country club
And gets to see his wife

Equal justice for all
They say it is the law
Equal justice for all
Who said only the indigent
Should be held at fault

Excess

Too much of anything
Is not good
A million of something
Knock on wood

Imagine yourself holding
A 100 pound weight
Trapped in a revolving door
For no escape

Excess gets you in trouble
Excess bursts your bubble

An overloaded truck
Pays per axle
A wealthy person
Pays even more taxes

Living the good life
Has limits
Being confined
Bars independence

Excess takes a toll
Excess is lost control

Exile

Baby, I realize you're still angry
About our disagreement the other night
I wish it never happened
You know I dislike to fuss and fight

I just can't seem to convince you
That I did not mean any harm and
No matter how hard I try
Of me, you don't want a part

You've got me in exile
Deported to some far away land
Lady, you put me in exile
Siberia was never this cold
The way you played your hand

If you would just write or call me
Tell me how I can make it up to you
I know we can work it out
Love will guide us through

I'll make love to you so good
Melt all the hurt away
The tears that you've cried will
Become a sunny day

Sweetheart, bring me back from exile
This desolate, lonely place
Exile is no man's land
Meanwhile, I'll dream of better bays

Extraterrestrial Love

The gods gave
Silent approval
From above

Knowing
I had your love

Nature's elements
Were there

A flash of lightning
Warmed the air

Rain pelted the ground
We were all around

Trees swayed
Back and forth

I am your love
You are my kettle of gold

We were at
The end of the rainbow

Find Them, Fun Them, Forget Them

He likes party girls
He doesn't want to marry
He likes to mess around
To have a cherry

He goes to singles bars
Even the local place
He picks the one he wants
You see it on her face

First he buys her a couple rounds
Then they dance to some songs
Next they make whoopee
Like a puff of smoke, he's gone

Find them, fun them, forget them
That is his only plan
Find them, fun them, forget them
1 night stands

He doesn't want phone numbers
Or know where you work
He wants no clues
He is just a flirt

You will find him wherever there's a party
Rapping to the fast ladies
That is his routine
For some serious playing

Find them, fun them, forget them
Night time flings
Find them, fun them, forget them
That is his only dream

Fire!

Baby, you keep a fire burning in me!
I am all aglow
You keep a fire burning in me!
I have never felt this way before

Into my abyss of darkness
You brought a beautiful light
With no more dark tomorrows
Or overcast yesterdays
You changed my life

You keep a fire burning in me!
A lantern that shines bright
You keep a fire burning in me!
Baby, you keep me hot during the night

My heart is filled with sunshine
You are the beacon that guides my way
Your brilliant love has brighten my mind
You will be my shining star always

You keep a fire burning in me!
Once an empty space
Baby, you keep a fire burning in me!
Look! Just look at my face!

Firing Line

I go to work
And I get bothered by the boss
When I arrive home
My woman yells at me
"You look like you're lost"

The bill collectors
Are always on my case
And my landlord is constantly screaming
"Son! Give up that check!"

I am on the firing line
I am getting hit from all sides
I am on the firing line
My life is on the line

I go to the store
But I can barely afford to buy
I have enough money for
Some pork and beans
But bread is sky high!

I want to run
To get away from it all
The creditors
Prowling in the shadows
Won't let me stray too far

I am on the firing line
There is no escape
I am on the firing line
Nobody I can pay

"Front Door Lover"

I don't like slipping and sliding
Joking or conniving-
Peeping and hiding

I don't want to be dibbling and dabbling
Half-stepping but grabbing
Or being called a back stabber

I want to be your front door lover
Not a back door man
I want to be your front door lover
No outside fad

You will not catch me

Skinning and grinning
Shaking or baking
Zigging but zagging
Skating and faking

I will never be

Hemming and hawing
Shucking or jiving
Bucking yet rearing
Banging and flying

I want to be your front door lover
Not a back door man
I want to be your front door lover
Not a thing from the past

I do not want to be

Flipping yet flopping
Boogying and bopping
Skimming but swimming
Jumping or hopping

I am not going to be

Huffing nor puffing
Running not gliding
Ducking or dodging
Tripping and hiding

I want to be your front door lover
Not your back door man
Make me your front door lover
I will keep you glad

To: MY From MWW May 22, 1997

Full Power

I am going to
Make love to you dear
And open up the throttle
I'm going to bear down
For relentless hours

I will turn on the after-burners
Undo the choke
I'll be using Class A jet fuel
Flame and smoke

Full power baby
Petal to the floor
Full power darling
Close the back door

I'll be your diesel engine
Rolling up the track
I'm aiming for
Your love tunnel sweetheart
To never look back

It's full speed ahead
Just like a bull
With tornado force
My sail will be full

I'm going to give you
Full power baby
Just like a Mack Truck
Complete power honey
I won't pass the buck

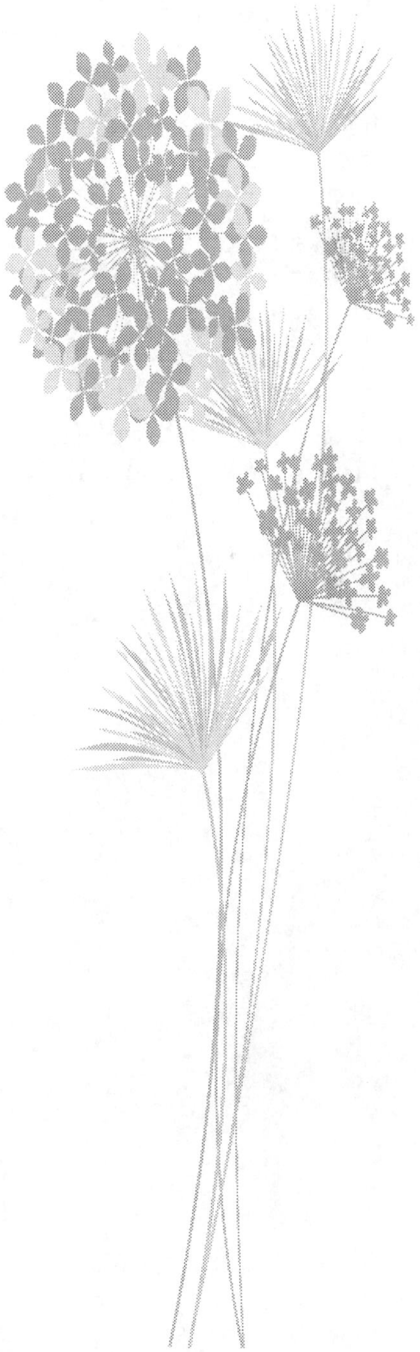

Funk!

Talking about funk

Baby, honey child let me tell you
About some funk . . .
Darling, I remember some funk
Back in 19 and 54

Child it was so funky
It knocked me through the door!

When I picked myself up—off the floor
I looked around and

The street sign said
Sixty-four!

Now that's FUNKEEEEEEEEEEEEEE Baby!
Funkier than 10,000 young jersey bulls!

10-4 Yall!

Genes

Why do I look like I do and
Act a certain way
Do these distinct characteristics
Make me have a patterned day?

Most situations I understand
Myself I cannot explain
I just don't comprehend
This information in my brain

Genes—have control
Genes—are my soul

I scan the earth
Searching for answers
Someday I believe
The solution will be my possession

Chromosome X and Chromosome Y
Can you please tell me
Who am I?

Genes—are mysterious
Genes—are my interior

Give Me Back My Towel

Give me back my towel
I'm not ready to give in
Give me back my towel
So that I can start my quest
For my goal to win

I want my towel back
So I can give life another shot
I want my towel back
To give life all I have got

I need my towel back
To come out on top
I need my towel
So that I will occupy
The number one spot

Give me back my towel
I am not ready to give up
I have found more than luck
Give me back my towel
My inspiration came from
High Above!

Glass Booth President

Seven times in two centuries
The chief executive has been fired on
Twice the assassins succeeded
Leaders forever gone

Legislation does not stop these killers
Criminals—their rights
With illegal weapons
It's just someone else's life

Put the president in a case
With all trust
Along with a megaphone
Secured on an armored truck

The glass booth president
Has come of age
The glass booth president
Maimers in rage

A campaign of sensibility
Puts the president's life on the line
With the responsibility of
Keeping the country in stride

The lone hunter
Relentlessly stalks his prey
As his fiendish nature
Drives him to hate

Put the commander-in-chief
Under lock and key
With a bullet-proof one-way mirror
No one will be allowed to see

The glass booth president
Survives day-to-day
The glass booth president
Four years his only way

Glitch

I was at the bench
Working on a chassis
When I looked up
Something went past me

It was fast as a flash
Quick as light
I tried to grab hold
But it was out of sight

They call him glitch
A smart little twit
They call him glitch
A swift son-of-a-bit

I wanted to catch the little bugger
So I took out my probe
I switched to 1000 nanoseconds
Then grounded the plug

I took a swipe
As he scooted past
He had a mind of his own
With emergency escape plans

I stepped up the probe current
To stun the little intruder
But he side stepped the probe
He was both clever and elusive

With a last ditch effort
I turned off the light
To get a better look
Then I saw him
Wave bye, bye
He was out of sight

Glitch—tiny twip
Glitch—speedy as whip

Go For It

You don't have to be a gopher
To give everything you've got
Take life with gusto
Give it your best shot

If there is something you want
Don't procrastinate about
Take your time and
You will end up without

Go for it!
Go, go, go!

Go for it!
Go, go, go!

Money should not be the object
Of your world pursuits
No amount of cash
Can see you through

Get on the stick
Full speed ahead
Don't ever look back
This race you will win

Go for it!
Hurry, hurry, hurry!

Go for it!
And don't you worry

Going Fishing

The elections are coming
Don't I have a choice
Away, I feel like running
I can't vote my voice

They tell me this is a democracy
Executed in republican ways
No matter what card I punch
I won't have a say

I think I'll go fishing
Maybe I'll just flip a coin
I think I'll go fishing
Surely, it would do no harm

I search, I compute
To choose the best candidate
Just who qualifies
When no one can pass the grade

Times of crisis
Should produce a leader
The nation needs solutions
Not indecision

I know I'll go fishing
Election day, I won't be around
Oh yes, I'm go fishing
No one deserves the crown

Goose Pimples

When you walk into a room
My heart starts to flutter
We touch
I melt like butter

We kiss
I begin to stutter
When we make love
You burst my bubble

Girl, you give me goose pimples
I want no other
You give me goose pimples
And sweet loving

I see you on the street and
My mind goes blank
I dream of you
You look so swank

I need you, honey
Just to think
I will keep you, darling
Like money in the bank

Baby, you give me goose pimples
Chills and fever
Goose pimples
Sweetheart, you are unbelievable

Myles W. Wallace

Ground Zero

There is no winning
In nuclear confrontation
The final result
-Total annihilation

The proliferation of weapons
Stockpiled by the world
Staggers the imagination
To be used just once

Ground zero is inevitable claim
Ground zero is madness, insane

The fallout would be absolute
Life could not exist
For those who survived
Nothing would be left

Every living creature
Would rapidly expire
This planet-earth
Would be engulfed in fire

Ground zero-
We need sound organization
To stop the craziness

Half Life

A young lady has a baby
Then daddy decides to leave home
With her child to raise
She is all alone

With the little one to nurture and
Memories of her lover still present
Her opportunity for a companion
Decreases by fifty-percent

With a half life
There is no time for entertainment
A half life is
Nature's rearrangement

Her education must continue
Although she has dropped out
She has to work seven days a week
And she feels left out

Baby is growing
And takes up most of her time
The toddler looks just like his papa
But baby is not his kind

A half life is
A period of assessment
Half life
Requires complete readjustment

Helicopter

I want a helicopter
To take from the top
I don't want a ladder
To flee the sparks

Fire escapes
They didn't build high
Leaping wouldn't be victorious
From up in the sky

Send the whirly birds in
Before the flames come
I don't need a blaze to
Assist my run

Helicopter, helicopter
Where are you at
My helicopter, helicopter
I can't use a net

Brother John, Mister Sears
You are both giant towers
A parachute isn't the way
For these untimely hours

I have got to be ready
If the inferno starts
A snorkel can't distinguish
From floor number one

Helicopter, helicopter
Glide on in
Say helicopter, helicopter
Where have you been

Helicopter, helicopter
This is first time I've wanted down
Hey helicopter, helicopter
Hurry up and bring me around

Hell Of A Weekend

Into work he strolled
His eyes were glazed-shut
His clothes were disheveled and
His hair a tangled mess

He sat down at his work space
He couldn't feel a thing
All he could think about was
The three day binge

His attempt to speak
Caused his lips to barely move
As far as he was concerned
He was still in the groove

It was a hell of a weekend, man
It was a hell of a weekend

Time stood still
As he tried to get his act together
His mind and body were
Totally discombobulated

He grabbed his tool
To give work a try
It was out of his control
Partying was his mind

His boss approached
And said: "What's the matter son?"
He tried to talk
But the cat had his tongue

It was a hell of a weekend, man
I mean it was a hell of a weekend

He struggled to his feet and
Groped for the door
His head was on cloud ten
His feet never touched the floor

His co-workers stared
They were taken aback
They thought they could have been
Part of the previous nights

He left the building
Ready to pass out
He never looked back and
With a whispered shout

He said:
"Yes sir, it was a hell of a weekend, man
A real hell of a weekend!"

Hip, Cool And Pretty

Go right ahead and be
Hip, cool and pretty
It doesn't require any skills
Go ahead and get high and
Act like Buffalo Bill

Go right ahead and be
Nickel and dime slick
Then ask yourself
Whose the trick

Go ahead and
Shoot people down
Then pick yourself
Off the ground

Go ahead on and
Try to whip the game
Knowing that it
Won't get you in
The hall of fame

Go right ahead and
Put on the whammy
Then see who gets
Knocked on his fanny

You think you are
Hip, cool and pretty
That is what you thought
Now you see that
Someone else is boss

Hog Head Cheese Blues

We are going to get you some fatback
We are going to get you some cone pone
We are going to get you some molasses
Don't forget those naked bones

That's just for starters:

We have candy yams
We have some crowder peas
We even have some
What do you call it
Dig in, roll up your sleeves

But first comes that good old
Hog head cheese
That's the main course and
We aim to please

For dessert we have pear preserves
In an old mason jar
We have some sweet potato pie,
Watermelon rind jelly and
Some peach cobbler pie

Now that your stomach is full
Let's top it of with
Some more hog head cheese
I told you it was good
Because we aim to please

Hot And Cold

Sometimes we make love and it's
Really out of sight
Other times we lay
I can't touch you all night

When we kiss
You make my lips sizzle
Then in the next moment
I can't get a nibble

You run hot and cold
Like electricity from a socket
Hot and cold
Like water from a faucet

Somedays you are total passion
And you don't want me to go away
Then other times
You just let the flame fade

Sometimes I hold your hand and
Feel a flaming pulsation
But in a short while
Your feelings are fluctuating

Baby, you run hot and cold
Just like winter's ire
Hot and cold
You are ice and fire

Human Being

I'm better than any machine
I'm a human being

I walk, I think
I can feel
I am a human being

Sometimes I dream of
Human beings

I don't have flashing lights
I do not speak a fancy language
I cannot be programmed and
I will not be rearranged

I am a human being

I celebrate
I smile
I touch
I was made from above

I am a human being

I Am A Prisoner In My Home

I can't go to bed at night
To get a minute of sleep
I rest with one eye open
There is never a moment of peace

The floodlights stay on
Both doors are bolted shut
The curtains are tightly drawn
And my equalizer is on my left

I am a prisoner in my home
I keep everything locked up tight
You see, I am a prisoner in my home
And I am ready to fight

People want to come in my house
When they were never invited
They want to take everything I own
And wonder why I become excited

It is a real shame
When you have to lock yourself in
It should be vice versa
Put the criminals in the pen

I am a prisoner in my home
I can't even go out
I am a prisoner in my own home
I can't even go out

I Am Your Man

I am your man
Let me lead the way
Take my hand
Today is an all new day

No use waiting in line
Men stand back!
I love this lady
This is no act

I am your man, sweetheart
Baby, don't you know
I am your man
You are the star in our show

No one will ever take your place
You will always be tops
That is the bottom line
My love you cannot stop

We were made for each other
I am your lighthouse of love
The love I have for you
Is guided from above

Darling, I am your man
Our love is so sweet
You are my world
You made my life complete

I Didn't Look Like Much

I don't look like much now
I didn't look much then
I came to fight
I came to win

The odds were against me
But I've stood the tide
It has been a rough road
I have my pride

Career? Woman? Car?
Money is not up to par
What's the answer to my problems?
A better job!

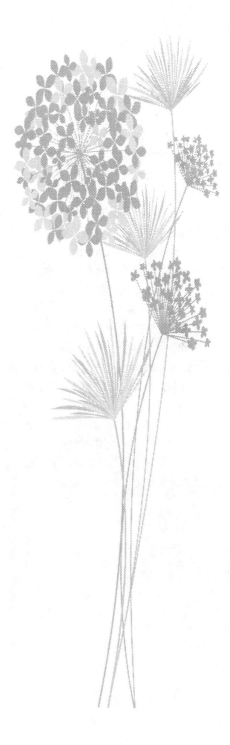

I Don't Want Nothing Old (But Money)

I don't want an old car or
An old set of clothes
I won't eat off of old dishes
I refuse to shop at old stores

When payday comes
I will take old bills
I like looking at Andrew Jackson
During the War-Civil

I don't want nothing old (but money)
And I mean a lot
I don't want nothing old (but money)
Bring to me by truck

I don't want an old lady
I don't want to live in an old pad
I don't need old furniture
I can't use an old plan

When it comes to the funds
Take it from the vault
I want to see plenty of money
So I can stand and shout

I don't want nothing old (but money)
Start with twenties
I don't want nothing old (but money)
And baby, keep it coming

I Have Seen Love, Heard Love, Spoke Love, But I have Never Had Love

Look at the loving couple
Strolling through the park holding hands
They appear completely satisfied
Their lives seem so grand

They are talking
Lyrical words they say
Their love looks beautiful
The birds begin to play

When I converse with friends
They tell me how nice it is to be involved
My response is one of bewilderment
They just nod and exhibit enormous smiles

I have seen love, spoke love, heard love
But I have never had love
I know my love would be sweet
I have seen love, spoke love, heard love
But I have never had love
My life is incomplete

Television presents me with only
Distorted shielded light
To view vague images
That flee from sight

When the radio station plays
Love on a two-way street
It leaves my heart to struggle
Once again with defeat

If my telephone rings
Which is only a misdialed number
Just as I answer—they hangup
My mind begins to flounder

I have seen love, heard love, spoke love
But I have never had love
I am too shame to deny
I have seen love, heard love, spoke love
But I have never had love
I ponder if love will pass me by

The skywriter paints a message
For those that share love
The bells toll
For couples that live love

Ministers marry many who have combined love
For me, I won't give in
As long as stars shine above

I have seen love, heard love, spoke love
But I have never had love
My love constantly escapes
I have seen love heard love, spoke love
But I have never had love
All I want is for
Love to be mine someday

I Know My Woman

She can be walking down the street
Or be riding in her car
She can be near yet
She can be far

Let me tell you thing
I know my woman

She can be wearing a dress
Or sporting a skirt
She can be wearing hot pants
With a see through mini-skirt

I'm telling you
I know my woman

I Know You Cried (Because I Did)

We had an argument
Then went our separate ways
Our disagreement lasted
Less than a minute
It seemed like it was for days

In the rain I walked
My heart was heavy
To see this hour come
I thought never

I know you cried (Because I did)
I felt your tears
I know you cried (Because I did)
Sweetheart, I need you here

With your absence
Life has not been straight
Drowning myself in alcohol
Is my only escape

If by some miracle
We get back together
I will hurt you no more
Love lasts forever

I know you cried (Because I did)
I was so happy with you
I know you cried (Because I did)
Darling, you love was true

I Present You

You are prettier than a picture
That came to life
You are beautiful as an angel
Twice as nice

You are sweet as honey
Pure of heart
Definitely a scholar
Three times as smart

You will be world renown
In a class by yourself
Lady you are so fine
Your love is wealth

I present you world, love

Myles W. Wallace

I Put The Fun In Funky

Do you want to get funky and
Have fun at the same time
Move straight ahead
To the front of the line

We're going to have some fun
While we have a good time
Because I put the fun in funky
Go ahead and taste the wine

Do what you want to do
Yeah, jump up and down
We're going to funk up the place
All over town

Grab yourself a partner
There is enough funk for two
We're putting the fun in funky
It's all up to you

I Want To Deserve Your Love

Baby, when I'm cranky
Keep away from me
Sugar, if I'm ornery
Just leave me be

I'm not the easiest person
To get along with
It will be difficult
Since together we're living

Bear with me, sweetheart
I will make everything right
The most important thing is
You stay by my side

I want to deserve your love
Honey, you're sweet and good
I want to deserve your love
I have misunderstood

It won't be an easy transition
Sharing our lives
I will do my best
I will try

I won't use excuses
Have faith in me
If I am not successful
Set me—free

I want to deserve your love
Soon I will
I want to deserve your love
Darling, stay with me till then

Myles W. Wallace

I Want To Make Love To You Everyday

I'm gone all week
Working five to five
When I come home on the weekends
I'm kind of tired

But, I don't want to sleep
I don't even want to lie down
All want to do is make love to you
Twenty-four times—the clock goes round

Even though I'm not home
To fulfill your requests
Goodness knows—in my heart
I'm trying to do my best

One minute of your love
Indeed it would be sweet
Even with one hour
My life would only be 75 % complete

It wouldn't be a roll in the hay
I want to make love to you everyday

Weekends come and weeks pass by
Fifty-two weeks make a year
But with your love
Any day is nice to have you near

You are so fine, baby
I want to make love to you everyday

I Want To Make Love With You (Not To You)

Together as one is
How we belong
Pulsating in unison and
Never apart

However we are positioned
I will be totally yours
Our jubilant involvement
Will be shared by both

I want to make love with you
(Not to you)
This special time will be only ours

I am going to make love with you
(Not to you)
These will be our greatest hours

Our bodies will blend and
Minds will combine
Inside of you
We will climax many times

We will shower in intimacy
Bath with sensuality
For the cleansing of our hearts
And healthiness of our lives

I want to make love with you
(Not to you)
To remain at our peak

I want to make love with you
(Not to you)
Darling, just you and me

I Want To Make Love With You (Not To You)

Together as one is how we belong
Spiralling in unison, never alone

However we are positioned
I will be totally yours
Our jubilant involvement
Will be shared by both

I want to make love with you (not to you)
Keep these moments ours
I want to make love with you (not to you)
To be our greatest hour

Torsos are mixed
Minds are twined
Inside each other for
The climax of time

We will shower in intimacy
Bath in sensuality
Our minds will be purified
To sensitize our hearts

I want to make love with you (not to you)
We will ride the wave past its peak
I want to make love with you (not to you)
Only you, just me

I Was Born On Independence Day

From Britain the United States
Formally seceded
July 4, 1776
My status as a person began
Prior to the country's nix

The constitution says
I became a citizen with
The Emancipation Proclamation in 1863
I say: Not true!
It is documented fallacy!

I was born on Independence Day
I was a man before 1619
I was born on Independence Day
Let freedom ring

My forefather fought to insure that freedom
Prevails in this country
Starting with the Revolutionary War
I raised my hand for freedom
During Viet Nam

The constitution states:
"All men are created equal
And people have the right to pursue
Life and liberty"

I was born on Independence Day
I am free!
I was born on Independence Day
Thank God Almighty
I am free!

I Won't Forget

Our coordinators leave in March
Martyrs for budget cuts
Business restructure
A numbers crunch

Field Service needs to feel
A local voice
Regional conversation
Cutbacks give no choice

Farewell to the women
Who dispatch calls
Goodbye ladies
To your jobs you gave all

I won't forget Connie
Responding with a smile
I won't forget Gina
Greeting me in style

I won't forget Chris
Beeping till I answer
I won't forget Diane
Always a happy camper

I won't forget
The new lady Cathy
Thank you all for being here
Memories will be everlasting

You will acquire new careers
Better positions yet
You made my life easy
I won't forget

Over the horizon
I see sunset
Without you ladies
It won't be the same
Good people I never forget

If Black People Love One Another (Why Do They Hurt Each Other)

In the year 1980 there were:

980 slayings in Detroit
890 lethal shootings in Chicago
2200 homicides in New York City

This is black on black crime.

We call are men brother
To the ladies we say: Hey sister!
Most us of hold jobs
To own homes we are persistent

Some of us have material possessions
We try to educate our children
Some of us go worship
But to others religion is unfamiliar

Then the paper reads:
Brother blows brother away
This something I can't figure out
Till this very day

We socialize together
By going to the same parties
We live in the same neighborhoods
We try to live hardy

Our lifestyles are similar
We like the same clothes
All of us want to get ahead in life
To our women we want to be close

But when you listen to the radio
You hear: Man does woman in
And you see it on television
When is it going to end

If black people love one another
(Why do they hurt each other)
When black people need one another
(How come they fight each other)

Jealousy and envy
Are spread throughout the human race
But we have more than our share
Someone is always trying to
Get on your case

Maybe it goes back to
When we were in bondage
And developed a self-hatred
Whatever it is
It keeps you wondering

You hear it from every acquaintances
Man did he hit her or
Someone fired a gun
Then we smoke, we drink
Just to go a little higher

We laugh, we joke
To try and clear our minds
We actively participate in sports to
Have a good time

As we play the game of life
With fierce determination
It is the same scene over and over
When we resort to primitive situations

If black people love one another
(Then why do we consistently suffer)
If black people love one another
(Why can't we help each other)

If In Doubt: Don't Do It!

You say you love her
You hardly ever call
Then you say you will visit her
Your mind is in the clouds

When you are in her
You tell her
You are the best you ever had
But when you aren't near her
You say you are so glad

If in doubt: Don't do it!
You will be using her
If in doubt: Don't do it!
You will be using her

You date others
But you never ask her out
She even gives you money
You say she doesn't count

Your feelings are on again, off again
More off, than on
You do not have time to vacillate
Before long, she will be gone

If in doubt: Don't do it!
You will no longer be using her
When in doubt: Don't do it!
You will only be losing her

If We Hadn't Met

I wish I hadn't met you
Not at this time
Two months from now
Would have been fine

I am in the process of
Getting myself together
I wonder if
We will ever come together

If we hadn't met
You wouldn't stay on my mind
If we hadn't met
You wouldn't be in my heart this time

Going from relation to relation
Causes significant problems
It is very difficult because
Hurt tends to follow

This situation makes me
Hold my feelings back
When I should reach out and try to
Keep our relationship intact

If we hadn't met
Would we have ever met?
If we hadn't met
Would I forget?

I'll See You In December

I met you in the summer
It was very, very hot
Now I find myself
Being a have not

I'll see you in December
When the air is fresh and cool
Because in the passion of summer
You played me for a fool

Heat was flowing all around
But I cried the tears of a clown

Winter is coming soon
To you, I'll be more than cool

Illusions

They seem so vivid
They go away
You could reach and touch
Distant like the Milky Way

Constantly emerging
But never near
No reason for fright
Nor fear

Maybe there is a heartbeat
The movements are soft
Petite

Step by step very close
Then suddenly . . . .
Always near, yet so far
A star

Close, close ever so close
To the brink or more

I'm A Vet

Just say my age is thirty
Although, I have lived
The life of one past forty

I have partied up
I have partied down
I have run through people
Left and right
Like hot butter on a knife

I have whipped the game
Both day and night
Without a bit of shame

I have run the streets
Hard and fast
But now that life has become
A thing of the past

I would like to meet the right one
Because I am ready to settle down
I should have taken Mom's advice
Every person is not a clown

Vet
Who me?
Ready to retire?
Not yet!

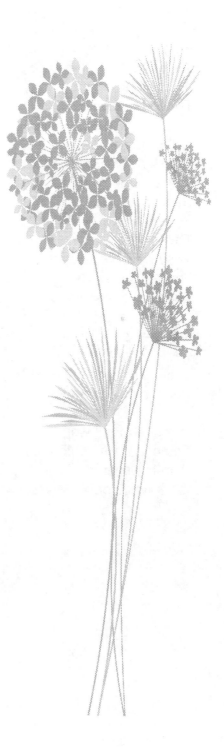

In The Name Of War

Look at your enemy
He looks just like you
Eighteen-years old
Fresh out of high school

Fighting a battle in
Which he had no choice
A no win situation
That has no voice

In the name of war
We shoot down our brothers
In the name of war
Sanctioned with orders

Those who return
They never recuperate
From this insanity
There is no escape

Old men sending young men
To do what they fear
Playing arm-chair-generals
Refusing to volunteer

In the name of war
The country's youth destroyed
With the shame of war
We have forsaken our sons

Include Me Out

If you want to raise sand and
Act a fool
Don't look at me
I'll be cool

Game playing
Is not my cup of tea
Stabbing people in the back
That's not for me

Include me out
If you talk about others
Include me out
Find another running buddy

Get your act together
Stand up—be a man
What you are about
Are not future plans

You are to people as
You perform to them
Stop acting silly and
Become somebody's friend

Include me out
If you don't want to do right
Include me out
Use my advice

Irrational World—Illogical Conclusion

April Fool's Day is appropriate
For what I'm going to write
So put your ears on and
Hold on tight

I have heard
What goes up, must come down
So I built up hope
Then before I knew it
Someone slammed the door

Today, I work harder
To make even less
Then they tell me
Things will get better, yet

It's an irrational world
Illogical conclusions
It doesn't make any sense
An irrational world
Illogical conclusions
And I don't have one red cent

I lived in a dream world
The first eighteen years
But when I got older
Life didn't have many cheers

I looked to the outer reaches
For some inkling of help
Then I found out, it's best
To look to myself

In an irrational world
Illogical conclusions
I don't understand the motive
This irrational world
Illogical conclusions
Will I ever get over?

Is There A Doctor In The House

My baby left me
I home all by myself
She went away weeks ago
And I haven't gotten better yet

She is always on my mind and
I don't know how to get her off
But I do know one thing for sure
Without her, I am a total loss

If she would just call
Is there a doctor in the house
She is my all
Is there a doctor in the house

I could check myself into a hospital
But I know she is my only cure
Even if I was an outpatient
She would be my medicine for sure

My world is shattered
I will never be the same
If she would only return
To relieve my pain

I will wait for her knock
Is there a doctor in the house
You see, my time is running out
Is there a doctor in the house

I've Got Something I Want To Tell The World (I Love You)

I could shout it from a house top
Or print it in the daily press
If I used a bullhorn
That would be better yet

I could get on the telephone
Perhaps the Internet
I'll send my message ship to shore
I'll say it whatever way is best

I've got something I want to tell the world
I love you

I've got something I want to tell the world
No one, I place above you

I'll spread my news across the sky
With the help of a G.E. Blimp
For what I have to say
No letter will they miss

I want to put my tidings in a rocketship
Send it into outerspace
I want the universe to know
Only you occupy my heart—my special place

I've got something I want to tell the world
I love you

I've got something I want to tell the world
All the galaxies too

We will walk together
Hand in hand
Our love for each other will be
Better than the promised land

No earthly force
Could ever tear us apart
Our bond will last forever
Longer than all the stars

I've got something I want to tell the world
I love you

I've got something I want to tell the world
I love you
You and only you

Myles W. Wallace

Know Yourself

To know yourself
Is to be yourself
Ego means me
It all says the same
You won't have to perceive

Difficult situations prevail
If you vacillate
You have got to be you
You do not come in triplicate

There are eyes watching
The game knows who you are
We are all bound together
Near and far

You may run
But not hide
The mirror of life
Reflects every side

Check yourself
You will be yourself
Love yourself
To be yourself

Kumquat

The room temperature was
One-hundred degrees C
Love making was everywhere
Generated by our breeze

We were working up a sweat
My baby and I were really getting down
When she whispered in my ear
Turn me around

Without hesitation
Quickly I proceeded
She relished my actions
Countering my speeding

My motions got faster
As I went in and about
Her eyes were glazed
When she began to shout:

"Kumquat!, Kumquat!"
I heard: "Come quick! Come Quick!"
She repeated: "Kumquat!, Kumquat!"
I toiled with my stick

This particular day, my honey wanted love
In an intricate kind of way
I was at her assistance
Twenty-four hours on that day

I gave her all the love
She ever needed
Her pleas of passion
Definitely were heeded

She spoke again:
This time, much louder than at first
"Kumquat!, Kumquat!"
Again I heard: "Come quick!, Come quick!"
I did exactly as she demonstrated
I came in her haven
Without reservation

Landlord

The ceiling leaks
The backdoor seeps

My neighbors sound as if
The place is on fire
And that is not
My most midnight desire

I lost one-thousand dollars
Worth of goods in theft
Then my landlord ripped me off
For what was left

Four rooms of heat in the summer
Come winter
And the warmth
Goes on a bummer

The ceiling caved in
While I was sleep
In came Mr. Hawk
Welcome back freeze

Some chump
Tried to fire up the place
And my mailbox was used
As the bait

I have got to move
Just as soon as I can
Even if it is to
A one-room shanty in wonderland

Last Part That Went Over The Fence

When I was coming up
Sunday's dinner was like a feast
I like to think about those good times
I come from a mid-sized family of six

We would have mashed potatoes
With peas and carrots
And of course gospel bird
Mom and Dad
Took the thighs and breasts
As for me

I got the last part
That went of the fence

My little sister consumed drumsticks
My brothers got the wings and back
By the time the bird got to me
Take a guess

I got the last part
That went over the fence

Now I am a man
I can buy most things I want
My upbringing tells me
To not overspend my budget

So when I dine out and
The waitress brings a large menu
I point to the very bottom and say

"Hey Miss, bring me

The last part
That went over the fence!"

Level Of Living

Some people survive in the projects
While others roam
Some reside in duplexes
Others do not have a home

The privileged live in penthouses
Nomads—uptown
Senior citizens reside in institutions
City fathers around town

There is level of living
Just like water can ascend
A level of living
Can make one depend

Some camp in tents
Others live in caves
It may be in an old log cabin
To be like Abe

Some stay in tenement houses
Others prefer row houses
Still others like town houses
My home is my house

There is level of living
Some live at the top
There is level of living
Some have bottomed out

Life (In A Needle)

Things are down and
You feel positive
It will pick you up
It is just the opposite

This dope
Is more destructive than fire
No good comes from it
Your mind is only higher

Life (in a needle)
Penicillin you cannot call
Life (in a needle)
Makes you think tall

A painless prick
Colorless—skin
On the ground-floating
Danger is near

Contamination is foregone
Mumbling, "I'm not hooked!"
You see yourself in a mirror
You did not look

Life (in a needle)
It is possible
Life (in a needle)
To get out of it

Liplock

When we kiss
My mind is fire
The sugar in your mouth
Ignites my innermost desires

We embrace
I don't ever want to let go
You are honey sweet
Lady, I am totally yours

Baby you put a liplock on me
You have the sweetest lips
Darling you put a liplock on me
You kiss so hep

Our tongues probe
It seems hours at a time
Our emotions tether
As we hold the line

Your kisses are like silk
With controlled warmth
The ambient moisture contains
Our flaming hearts

Baby you put a liplock on me
Kissing you is all delight
Sweetheart you put a liplock
I could kiss you every night

Living, Learning, Loving

The sun rises
To reclaim a new day
Earth blossoms
Sprinkled by oceans waves

Each drop of dew
Brings forth surrealistic images
A profound display
Of a prolific beginning

I am living, learning, loving
About life presents
I am living, learning, loving
About universal consequences

I see magnificent flowers
I feel tranquil thoughts
The wind reverberates
For earnest beauty—sought

Time only heightens
These joyful visages
Night reproduces
These stellar lineages

I am living, learning, loving
Truly this is a dream
I am living, learning, loving
Or is it real?

Loneliness (You're A Friend No More)

In a cold room I sat
Empty beer cans surrounded me
The window shades were tightly drawn
Darkness lurked persistently

I was afraid to move
I was terrified beyond reason
Courage I could not build up
There was nothing but indecision

Indecision gripped me like vise
It held me unyieldingly
No one I could turn to and
Expose my feelings

Although we hadn't know each other long
I felt something, right from the start
With lingering desire
You—I wanted to be a part

When the telephone rang
I answered to hear your sweet voice
Off the floor I rose
To be your only choice

Loneliness (you're a friend no more)
Not since my baby
Loneliness (you're a friend no more)
We will keep you away together

Sunlight now shines in my home
From your glowing heart
My door is always open so that I can
Greet you with waiting arms

I will continuously serenade you
With flowers and candlelight
You changed my way of living
You gave me a better life

Your kind of loving
Has to be the master's plan
We reached the plateau of love
Without you, I would not have attained
Success, no doubt, is yours to claim

Loneliness (you're a friend no more)
Your time has come and gone
Loneliness (a friend no more)
To the past you belong

Love (You Are My Poem Come True)

Through thoughts and wishes
I dreamed of "Lady Fair"
One who is considerate
Devoid of flair

By chance we met
If by design
Joy you brought
Into this life mine

Love (You are my poem come true)
Just like a genie's wish
Love (You are my poem come true)
Your love is heaven sent

Beautiful you are
Woman-child
My life you complete
Near or far

Inseparable
Are our bonded minds
You are my cinderella
Sugar so fine

Our vivid love
Paints the sky
Hand in hand
With rainbow hearts

The love we express
Is from inside out
The only place
That love counts

Love (You are my poem come true)
My magical baby
Oh, love (You are my poem come true)
Our love is beyond my imagination

Love Waits For Me

On the other side of a rainbow
At the end of an abyss
Close to the seashore
Appears my dream
Love waits for me

On the mountain peak
Near the valley base
My heart speaks
A passion plea
Love waits for me

On the edge of twilight
The threshold of hope
The metronome of romance
Counts increase
Love waits for me

Where grass is green
Life is sun
Cupid's arrow lands
To blossom
Love waits for me

Make Myself A Chicagoan

While visiting Chicago
From another state
I have grown to like it here
I am going to put down some roots
Because this city is dear

I will acquire the style
I will develop the walk
I will buy a nice car
And learn the talk

I am going to make myself a Chicagoan
Chicago is my kind of town

I am going to make myself a Chicagoan
I will tell every person I meet
About the city proud

I'll live on the southside
Where there is plenty of action
I will find a home
Soon I'll start packing

I will find a good job
And discover a nice lady
I will pursue my dream
Everything will be great

I am going to make myself a Chicagoan
I will be real cool

I am going to make myself a Chicagoan
I will have the tools

Middle-Class

They walk their poodles
With their mouths up-side-down
Their lives are on a limb
They never smile

Mother and father both work
Along with brother and little sis
One day from their jobs
They dare not miss

Education is a commodity
They cannot afford
They break their backs
Just for room and board

The middle-class
Have two-cents over their carfare
The middle-class
Have gel in their hair

Mortgage payments
Eat up most of their checks
The rest is spent on
Keeping up with the Joneses
Their next door neighbors

They run from poverty
They forgot from where they come
Riding in their Mercedes
In a minute they'll pass you up

At their social gatherings
The champagne glasses are
Held by the stem
They listen to Bach and Beethoven
Thinking of B.B. King

Being middle-class
Is a mental condition
Being middle-class
Is a deficiency admission

Minority—Who Me

I pay my taxes
I work everyday
With the high price of gas
I have earned my way

I take care of my children
I cloth and feed
To me they come for
Anything they need

Minority—who me
I am six feet tall
Minority—who me
I stand proud

In community affairs
I actively participate
I am a registered voter
The president I elect

My mortgage
Is not overdue
I got my education
From hard work school

Minority—who me
I am in the majority
Minority—who me
I am uniformity

Miss America

I am a strong woman
A proud woman
I am not a gaud woman
Or a child-woman
I am Miss America

I am not influenced by society
In what the definition of a woman is
I walk with my head held high
I always perform to win
I am Miss America, Miss America, Miss America

My lips are full
My skin is brown
My eyes are pretty and round
I am built firm all around
At others I never frown
I am Miss America

I am a leader in the world
I place my family first
I don't try to keep up with the Joneses
Sometimes I hurt
I don't ever want to convert
I am Miss America, Miss America, Miss America

I expect the best from life
I work hard to acquire
I look good for my man
It is he, I most desire
I am black, I am proud
I am Miss America, Miss America, Miss America

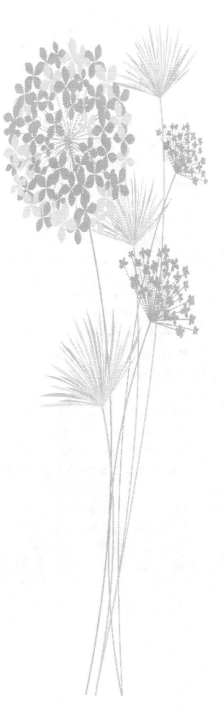

Myles W. Wallace

Money And Power

Money and power
Go hand in hand
Money and power
The rule of the land

When you grow up poor
You don't have many dreams
You just work real hard
To try to make ends meet

But in your mind
You know it is a lie
All you want is money and power
You want to control the sky

You rob and steal
You do it in an orderly way
They call it embezzlement
Then you have all the say

You rise to the top
Forgetting all your friends
You don't want to see anyone
Not even your kin

As quickly as you ascended
You soon bottom out
You end up beneath where you started
It's called being down for the count

Money and power
Was your downfall
And to think
You thought you had it all

My Ancestors Were Slaves

You call me dumb
Say I cannot read or write
Look at me
Our jobs are the same type

You tell me I will never learn math
I will never fly a plane
I am a General
From the Air Force Academy, I came

My ancestors were slaves
What were yours
My ancestors were slaves
Don't you know

Your ancestors kept us out of school
My people lived in the fields
Our unpaid labor
Paid your bills

Our only social function was
The exercise of religion
Which kept our heads together and
Gave us vision

My ancestors were slaves
What's your answer
My ancestors were slaves
Is that out of the question

My Life, My Love, I Give You My Everything

I live my life just for you
You make my world turn
My sun to view

You are sweetness
The morning rising
You are the sunset
On my horizon

You make the stars
Twinkle in the night
Without you
I would not have daylight

The moon is always full
With you
Radiating with
Shimmering beauty

My world would not exist
Without you
You keep my life
So refreshingly new

Never Too Old To Party

Get out of that rocking chair
Away with the specks
It is time to get down
For goodness sakes

Off with the slippers
Make yourself dap
It's time to be funky
Toss the stocking cap

You're never too old to party
Your dues have been paid
You're never too old to party
It is time to play

Start jamming
Let yourself go
You will be the star
In your own picture show

Make today
The best of your life
Glide with the beat
While you sip some wine

You're never too old to party
Move those feet
You're never too old to party
Look, you're creating a scene

Nobody To trust, No One To Love

I left home
At an early age
No one was there to guide me

Now, as an adult
It is more—the same
I need someone beside me

Nobody to trust, nobody to love
The story of my life
Nobody to trust, nobody to love
I need advice

I am a wanderer
Just who am I?
I have no destiny
Life's messages I don't identify

The tunnel's light
Awaits my touch
I reach out—but
I can't hold long enough

Nothing But A Star

The lady I marry
Make her a star
My lifetime I have waited
To be a part

I want to wake in the morning
Look at her lovely smile
I like going to bed and
Doing it in style

Nothing but a star
That is all I want
Nothing but a star
One who is choice

I know she will be sweet
And genuinely nice
She will love me
She will give me advice

She will not flirt
With her I will never be alone
She will be my company
When she's not at home

Nothing but a star
That is how I feel
Nothing but a star
Someone real

O.D.

You start on something mild
You are looking for a thrill
You don't really care
If you are taken to the hill

You say you are doing this
Because in it is hope
Of course you know
You won't find that with dope

But anyway you continue
And get on something hard
You seem to be looking for
Your number in the cards

Now you're to the point
To no one you can turn
Because of you,
Through you—they will learn

Finally the moment comes
You take the giant step
In it goes
There is no retreating
Please help

Oats And Crow

He swaggered into the room
With his chest stuck out
He had beltless pants and
His sandal toes—poked out

Selling wolf tickets
He thought he was the duke
Epithets rolled off his lips
Further agitating his snarled mood

His target of intimidation
For sure—me
His continuous diatribe
Was loud and offensive could be

Something gave him the perception
I might be a chump
What he didn't know was
I could whip his natural but

Feeling his oats
Soon he would be eating crow
Feeling his oats
I would slam the back door

In my face
That's where he was
Shooting off his mouth and
Getting on my last nerve

I tried to be cool
I didn't want to make a scene
This dude was performing-
Pure make-believe

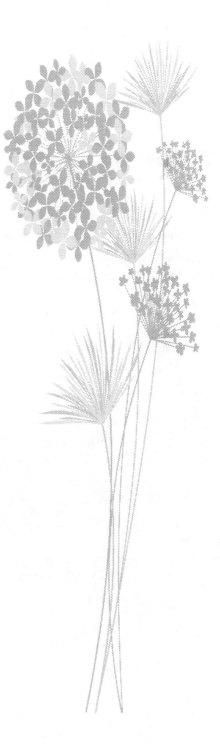

He wouldn't back down
Then he raised hand and
Aimed it at my face
But it didn't land

I blocked it with a left
Lashed out with my right
I was fired up and
Thought about my knife

Common sense prevailed
As the bully pleaded from the floor
I let him slide
He said he couldn't take it anymore

Feeling his oats is
Something he won't do anymore
Feeling his oats
He ate the whole crow

Old Men

They chase young girls
To recapture youth
With their grown children
They teach different pursuits

The game they play
Hurts all involved
Just to prove
They are men about town

Old men
Full of flame and fury
Old men
Signifying nothing

They pull in front of schools
With their ten-year old caddies
Retired from life
With nothing to do better

Like a fox
They steal new chickens
Yesterday's would-be casanovas
Destroy all ambitions

Old men
Dancing to an old tune
Old men
That will fade soon

One Eye Bandits

Those one eye bandits
They terrorize people on the roads
One eye bandits
Streets they think they own

The cars they drive
Have only one headlight
They look like a one-eye brutes
On the highways at night

You think they are motorcycles
When you go off to the shoulder
They just keep coming at you
They are little more bolder

If you see them speeding
Flying over a hill
The quicker you move
The better they feel

One Fell Swoop Of Your Love

Out of the clear blue sky
You came like a hawk in pursuit
Talons stretched out
To run was of no use

Though I never stumbled
Nor did I sway
I seemed, someway, somehow
To be your only prey

One fell swoop of your love
I knew I would be captured
One fell swoop of your love
I was enraptured

The summer winds that day
Caused your sweet smell
To permeate the air

Your graceful beauty
Descended on me
My attraction was
More powerful than gravity

Your arms were like wings
That held me firm
Your body soft as feathers
Was filled with warmth
My heart began to sing

One fell swoop of your love and
The seed of love had been planted
One fell swoop of your love
Made my love grow faster

One If Day, Two If By Night

I know you are married
Living with a man
I will never forget you
Not long—I can

When your telephone rings
You will know it is me
I am still around
For you, I will always be

Ring, one if by day
You are in my heart
All that I need

Ring, ring, two if by night
Your good love-
Memories too sweet

At the office
All my thoughts are of you
I am without recuperation
I don't want to meet anyone new

I walk the streets and
I look into telephone booths
I hold your number close
It is the loving truth

Ring, one if by day
Without you I am not connected
You stay on my mind

Ring, ring two if by night
I want to be with you
Till the end of time

Only In America

Only in America
Can a man be called boy
While they turn soldiers into toys

Only in America
Could we have Jerry Ford
And 10,000,000 unemployed

Only in America
Could we let Nixon escape
The chief conspirator of Watergate

Only in America
Could we shoot down a King
And let the Liberty Bell ring

Only in America
Can the poor starve
Just ask Agnew what is a harvest

The good old U.S. of A.
Is where you don't get paid
If you decide not to play

America is where children get bussed
Look at the 3-piece suit executives
Make such a fuss

America is where the old get exiled
And committees smile

America, is where we wave flags
It is a amusing because
We never looked at the tag

America, America take a look and
You will see
You are nothing like
You were meant to be

Our Love Has Burnt Out

The searing, seething, surging feeling
We once knew—has grown old
There are only embers, cinders, ashes
Love glows no more

Our candle light romance
Has found the end
We went from torrid to cold
It seems so wicked

Our love has burnt out
Light flickers no more
Our love has burnt out
There is no kindness in store

The kissing, holding, caressing
Has come to a halt
There are only negative, numbing, notions
That made our love fall

The prismatic rainbow we had is
No more fulfilling
Our present situation
Has minds unforgiving

The heat
We felt at the start
Has lost its mystic
There is no spark

My love has burnt out
No longer is it in my heart
Your love has burnt out
Of me you don't want a part

Our Women

Our women are the way they are
Because that is way nature
Intended them to be
Just imagine if they
Performed like you and me

Could you see our ladies
Not having babies
Or how about our women
Not giving away any

What if they acted like
They didn't have good sense
Or gossip with the neighbor
Across the fence

What if the were not
Soft to the touch
With lips to kiss
An absolute must

And what if they didn't cry
And be so fine
And didn't meet you at the door
To ask you for
A little bit more

Out Of Order

When I call you a recording says
The phone is disconnected
Numerous letters I write
But the mailman says you've relocated

When I do see you
You tell me you can't come over
Because your car broke down

And you can't use your bike
Because parts haven't come
From out of town

You are out of order
Like a broken faucet
You are out of order
A damaged outlet

I thought our union
Locked out all reservations
Now you say
We didn't have the right combination

I just knew our romance
Was headed to the top
But it skidded to a halt
And the bottom dropped out

You are out of order
Like a faulty tumbler
You are out of order
Just like a leaking awning

Overachiever

He can win the race in three
He does it in two
He shows everyone up
With nothing to prove

He is good, maybe great
But it has gone to his head
Modesty is not his virtue
Ego is instead

The overachiever can have his day
The overachiever always wants his way

To the top he rises
More rapidly than others
After reaching his goal
He wants to go further

The peak may be all his
Satisfaction he will never win

The overachiever has a peacock's pride
The overachiever is unhappy inside

Phony Laugh

When I tell a joke
You want to cry
Inside you hurt
With giggling you hide

When we go to the movies
There can be a mystery showing
You burst out grinning
If the lights are lowered

With a phony laugh
You cannot be yourself
The phony laugh
Gets no respect

I realize you feel like
Life has let you down
But a frown is no more than
An up-side-down smile

There are times when I feel
You want to run away
Just remember the Sun shines
Even on rainy days

I will help you to
Discover your inner self
Elevate your pride
Make yesterday second best

That phony laugh will become
No more than a trickle
Never will a phony laugh
Make you tickle

Player

He is single
The man lives alone
He has a roll-away bed
With a portable phone

He meets young ladies
Who have many friends
Then he gives an affair
And romances all of them

They call him player
The life of the party
They call him player
He just laughs heartily

He says the ladies
Just have fun
And drink some wine
He says it is just frivolity
Then draws the line

Festivity is ok with him
He says he is only a man
He just tries to
Get as must as he can

He is a player
He just wants to play women
Yeah he is player
He says next; a harem

Playing Hard To Get

When I call
You are always gone
You tell me to come by
When you are not alone

We make a date and
You never show
I want to go and party
You say take it slow

You are playing hard to get
Like a pass to a receiver
Playing hard to get
You smart deceiver

You are more illusive
Than Harry Houdini
You disappear for weeks
I only see you if I am dreaming

You make an appearance
To keep me in check
Then, away you go
Leaving me a nervous wreck

You are playing hard to get
You little heart stealer
You are playing hard to get
You clever wheeler dealer

Pride

Pride:
Pride is
Standing up
For what you believe
Pride is
Saying thank you
Please

Pride is
Never giving up
Pride is a job
Well done

Pride is
Sacrifice
Pride is
Being nice

Pride is
Faulting no one
Pride is
Helping someone

Pride is
Facing adversity
Pride is
Having tenacity

Pride is
Inside
Pride is
To shine

Myles W. Wallace

Profiles In Courage

There's a man
Who cannot see
He has inner vision
Reality like you and me

There's a lady
Sitting in her chair
She can only move her fingers
Knitting at the county fair

Profiles in courage
Examples—two
Profiles in courage
Excellent views

There is a child
And he is ill
He manages his wagon
Up the hill

Here's an athlete
Who is in traction
His mind is
On the action

Profiles in courage
Never give up
Profiles in courage
Heroes: Those above

Profit

Profit to some people means to
Make as much money as one can
Even if it involves
Terminating workers
To keep a company in the red
They do what is bad

Some firms could care less about
The people they run over
Mortgages, child support,
Food, shelter and clothing
Don't mean a thing
When corporate profits
Represent nothing but greed

Profit over the well-being of people
Is a crime against all humanity
To put profit above people
Is total insanity
How can business be so inconsiderate!

If this foolishness continues
Consumers will revolt
Companies need to stop sending
Jobs abroad and
Take care of workers at home first
Coast to coast

Profit over people
Is a repugnant revelation
Profit replacing people is
Boardroom persuasion
That reveals executives are
Absolutely crazy!

Profit higher than people
Provides workers only with acute pain
Profit beyond people is endless shame and
Business deserves all the blame

Myles W. Wallace

Put It Your Bootie

Move your body
Up and down
Twist your hips
In, around

Pump energy
Below your waist
Find your feet
A solid base

Put it in your bootie
Just like a shot
Put it in your bootie
Fire hot

Put it in your bootie
Like a bow
Put it in your bootie and
Let it flow

Break the barrier
A sonic boom
Explode-
Shudder the room

Fluid poetry
Spiralling waterbed
Painted spinning top
Straight ahead

Put it in your bootie
Packed like a cannon
Put it in your bootie and
Make love fantastic!

Put The Ball On The Wall

Tear them down
Blast them away
They were not built
To last forever anyway

Put the ball on the wall yall
Put the ball on the wall you all
Put the ball on the wall
Put the ball on the wall yall

Reduce them to rubble
Turn them to bricks
They are eyesores
For living they are unfit

Put the ball on the wall you all
Put the ball on the wall yall
Put the ball on the wall
Put the ball on the wall you all

Slum buildings
Must torn down
Ghetto dwellings
Do not belong in town

Construct modern homes
People need more space
Give them a chance
To escape the ratrace

Put the ball on the wall yall
Put the ball on the wall
Put the ball on the wall you all
Put the ball on the wall!

Racism

Racism is: When O.J. Simpson can be convicted
Without having all the facts
When Rodney King is "resisting"
Laying flat on his back

Racism is going to your bank
To try to obtain a loan
Then wonder whether-
You will ever own a home

Racism hurts, racism destroys
Racism is immoral and cowardly
It is men becoming boys and
Racism is their toy

Racism steps on all that are involved
Both oppressor and victims
Racism has no business being
A part of any business or personal experience

Racism must be halted
Racism must cease
Down with racism
Up with hope and dreams
We are all human beings

Racism will only be stopped
When everyone becomes involved
Put a stop to racism
Let us start right now!

Ransom For Love

Our romance was strong
Life was—great!
We were at the pinnacle of love making
Our relationship was solid that day

We were about to fulfill our dream
But, before that special moment came
You hit on me to become your sponsor
My life will never be the same

It was not a fortune that
You wanted advanced
You didn't say what it was for
But, you told me if I did not come through
Lovemaking would stop

You wanted ransom for love
You placed a value on emotions
With ransom for love
You abducted all my devotion

I am not opposed to giving you money
We all have our needs
But, you backed me against a wall and
You took away my feelings

I finally gave in
To your brazen request
I thought this would put as back together
My heart knew
It wouldn't even be temporary

Going against my will
Made me feel, less the man
I haven't completely gotten over you
You just don't fit into my plans

You wanted ransom for love
Money for rendered services
With your ransom for love
You made your love self serving

Right On

Right on brother
You did what
You were supposed to do
They ran after you
Wild beasts escaped from a zoo

You were marching
For what is fair
Human Rights that vanished
Right into thin air

They came at you
With truncheons drawn
You knocked them down
To the ground
They lay scattered all around

And now you stay
On the row
Praying that justice
Will come forth

Your fate could be resolved any day
Until then, you wait
Although, it is touching to say
Your destiny was decided yesterday

Run

Run, yeah run just fast as you can
Run, run without taking my helping hand
Run, go ahead and run
Run until you fall out
Run, run, run, if you think
That is what life is about

Keep running until
You run out of gas
Run just run
Right back to your past

Yeah run, just run until
You are out of steam
Keep on running
Right through your dreams

You can run to the east
You can run, run to the west
Just keep running
Without trying to your best

You can run
Until you turn blue
You are only running
Just from you

You can run near and
You can run far
Just keep running
Back to my arms

Sad Eyes

Sad eyes all around
Sad eye—Uptown

Sad eyes asking questions
Sad eyes reveal uncertainty

For moments of happiness
They would surely wink
With hours of gloom
They don't even blink

They have not given up
Opportunity will strike
They will latch on
To never turn back

Sad eyes full of hope
Sad eyes show soul

Sad eyes see above
Sad eyes are love

Safety Is, Is As Safety Does

Safety should be the concern of
All companies' constituents
Since every employee can be
A Safety Representative

There should be no procrastinating
Since safety starts at home
Then continues at work
Where safety can be observed every minute
Without mistakes or quirks

Use safety around equipment
Use safety with tools
Be safe with electricity
Use safety with every job you do

Safety is, is as safety does
Perform safely all the time
Safety is, is as safety does
Safety is the top of the line

Safety insures that the day is good
With safety there is no need to knock on wood
Safety is the only sure way to go
Safety does everyone good

Safety is, is as safety does
Safety is never a given
Safety is, is as safety does
With safety, everyone is a winner

♥ Secret ♥

What is this secret you carry around
That you don't want anyone to know
What is this secret you keep
That you won't let yourself go

Your conversations are always brief,
Straight to the point
You won't let them flow

Your visits are quick and
You are always in a hurry to
Rush out the door

What is your secret
Please tell me
I won't tell anyone else

I want to know your secret
So that I can put
My sanity to rest

Did you hit the lotto?
Your ship came in?
Are you going away
To never come back again?

Does it involve business?
Is it a personal condition?
Or is it a new investment?
Possibly a romantic situation?

I have got to know your secret!
I have to know it right now!
Not knowing your secret
Keeps my mind in a cloud!

♥

She Never Said I Love You

She never said I love you
Although she showed me in so many ways
She never said I love you
She sparkled with love day after day

She never uttered one single word about love
Her love was from high above
Even her lips didn't reveal the act
Her love was always fact

She never said I love you
Her expression would never stray
She never said I love you
Her emotions were not that way

She will always love me
Though silent as a breeze
In her heart
I will always be her king

She's Pretty—But Can She Make Love

I met this lady
Stacked—head to toe
Could she get down
I had to know

I invited her over, we talked and
I offered her some wine
Shortly thereafter
I knew she was mine

She's pretty—but can she make love
I wondered as I looked into her eyes
She's pretty—but can she make love
I would know in time

We kissed
Man she was sweet
We hugged
I felt so complete

Intimate we became
I reached my peak
One second later
She was in ecstasy

Sweat poured
We screamed simultaneously
Delicious she was
A part of me

She's pretty—but can she make love
A most definite yes!
She is beautiful and she can make love
That's no guess

Sister Humble

She was a senior member of
The Cathedral of Love
Where she lived round the clock
No matter where you were
Bifocals watched

She wore cluck heeled shoes
A starched white dress
Always fanning and
Ready to inspect

Sister Humble
No games she played
Sister Humble
Gave no breaks

Talking in Sister Humble's house
Was forbidden to do
She better not catch you sleep
Because she'd whip on you

A firm believer in the good book
She was a worshipper of rules
You didn't let her hear you laughing
She was no ones fool

Sister Humble
Had a hawk eye
Ole Sister Humble
You dare not try

Small Talk

It starts when you go to work
It doesn't stop till you leave
Sometimes you want to run and hide
Pretend it is make-believe

They can't leave well enough alone
They have to complicate matters
They have to make the story real juicy
It all amounts to mindless chatter

Small talk, you know how it goes
Small talk, no one smells like a rose

The subject can be anything and everything
Which amounts to nothing really
You ask them for their comments
And they say something silly

It goes on constantly
It follows you like a shadow
Whether day or night
It is about situations
That don't even matter

You can't get away from it
You hear it everyday
From this dialogue
It is easy to walk away

Small talk, that's what I'm talking about
Small talk, is it worth writing about?

So You Want To Be A Temptation

The Temptations are an institution
Not just another group
They put on brilliant performances
Send you back to school

To be a member
You have got to sing and dance
But more than anything
Pass their test

Get in line
Do the choreography
Croon your heart out
Use some strategy

So you want to be a Temptation
Think you are good enough
You want to be a Temptation
Show your stuff

Put on your tuxedo
Wear it in style
Light up the stage
With a million-dollar smile

Do the Temptation Walk
One-fifth the harmony
Entertain well enough
To win several Grammies

So you want to be a Temptation
Think you are in their class
You want to be a Temptation
You have got to be bad
Real bad!

Society Wants Me / But Doesn't Let Me

Society says—smile!
Yet gives me a hard time
Society tells me to act intelligent
Then draws a line

Society yells—get a job!
Work is hard to find
It is minimum wage or else
Do some time

Society wants me / but doesn't let me
Anything that I do is inconclusive

Hey wait a minute: I have a solution!

I do not care if society
Does not like what I do
I will do what I please
I will be real cool

I will dance and party
Have a good time
When I feel like it
I will taste some wine

My forbearers were forced to compromise
They broke their backs
Just to survive

Society wants me / but doesn't let me
I do not care
Society wants me / but doesn't let me
Society is not fair!

Somewhere Down The Line (You Will Love Me)

Why don't you come by my house
I mean my apartment
I said my room
I am staying with friends
Because I'm down and out

A Mercedes you drive
I have a push-mobile
If your does not start
I will be there to
Transport you uphill

Although I am on my last leg
And you are at the top
I need you here now
To share your warmth

You are beautiful, famous and rich
I am just a man
I love you
One day you will understand

Because, somewhere down the line
You will see my love as true
Some where down the line
My love is special, just for you

A college education you have
I am just a high-school grad
I have seen your class ring
Something I have never had

You work in a glass tower
I am a clerk in a five and dime store
You dine out every night
Coupons litter my kitchen floor

Somewhere down the line
(You will love me)
I will stay in your sight
Somewhere down the line
(You will love me)
Because, you are my life

Speed

I like swift planes
And flashy cars
That run 200 miles per hour
Just to start

I dig rapid trains
Sailing boats
Racing cycles
I want the most

I want speed
Quicker than a spark
Yeah speed
Two to three mach

I am crazy for the silver streak
I dream of the bobs
The tilt-the-whirl—my favorite
I revere the parachute dive

Water skiing
Ah! The blue-hued sky
Plunging sunsets
They really catch my mind

I dig speed
I mean smoking!
Yeah speed!
And I am not joking!

Myles W. Wallace

Stand Fast With Your Love

You say you love her
She tells you to give up
Constantly she rejects you
Says you aren't good enough

Don't throw in the towel
Love just doesn't go away
And don't give in
Love her more everyday

Stand fast with your love
Patience will see you through
Stand fast with your love
She is just getting to know you

You call, you write
But your messages go unanswered
The love you have for her
You want it to be everlasting

Keep plugging away
Don't give up the ship
She can't continue to deny your love
Your feelings she will miss

Stand fast with your love
Keep holding on
Stand fast with your love
Romance will be yours before long

Starring You

The curtains open
Starring you
The flood lights shine
Starring you

You are a thespian and
You appear on my matinee
You belong on every set
I desire you for every play

The theater is yours
The platform concerns you too
The scene is one of romance
As we begin act ii

This is our greatest performance
Starring you
Better than Shakespeare
Starring you

The role will always be yours
You were cast as new
The script contains lines
Developed only for you

The skit is simple
Accompanied by a symphony
Your walk on presentation
Will be proceeded by a timpani

The curtains part
Starring you
The floodlights shine
Starring you

Sterile World

They come from where
Man and wife
Together they don't sleep
How their children came
It is a mystery

Their children go to
The best schools and
The parents don't know
The golden rule

Other kinds of people
Are not good enough
Being the way they are
Is repulse

Stop This Madness!

Nuclear proliferation
Atomic bombs
Surface to air missiles
Crippling guns

Radar patrolling space
Humans displaced
Push button generals
Ratrace

Stop this madness!
Quit! Halt! Cease!

Stop this madness!
Give the world peace!

Men ordered to fight
Foreign land
Hand to hand combat
Man for man

Military revenue
Conference table
Mature are the willing
Young are the able

Stop this madness!
Retreat to our senses!
Stop this madness!
Protest intervention!

Stunned

My honey revealed
She was living with another man
That threw a wrench into
My master plans

I wanted my baby and I
To move into the same house
But she said she couldn't
And told me to get lost

I am stunned
As if I was stung by a bee
Like I ran into a tree

I am stunned
We never negotiated
Pain I never anticipated

The real story is: In this home
She wanted brand new furnishings
Which I couldn't afford
With the money I was earning

She was not working
I told her: "Find a job"
That's when she left me
She didn't want to hear my line

I am stunned
I have lost my lady
I haven't recuperated

I am stunned
I am all alone
My house never became a home

Take Care Of Your Body

You only get one
Duplicates cannot be made
Unlike machines
Your body will not be replaced

You have to feed and nourish your body
Just like you align and lubricate a car
Give yourself the best ingredients
So that you can go far

Take care of your body
You are allowed only one per customer
Take care of your body
You will receive no other

Keep away from needles
Do not consume pills
Extravagant liquor is a definite way to
Go over the hill

Milk and cookies
May sound humorous to you
For sure these ingredients
Will see you through

Take care of your body
Do not let your body go down
Take care of your body and
Your body will keep you around

Teacher

As a grown man
I thought I knew all
There was to know
When you revealed to me
There was still room
For me to grow

You started with
My personal appearance
Which I admit was second best
But, with your careful attention
I now stand tall among the dressed

You taught me
There is more to life
Then sitting in the house
And listening to the stereo
Or watching television
I sincerely appreciate your concern
You have made my life
Immensely pleasurable

You taught me how to
Love my family
Especially my mother
The same way you feel about your Mom
You gave me lessons in
How to love you as a woman
No other had I loved before
And no one else do I want to be a part

I call you teacher
Not because you are
An instructor of kids
I call you teacher
Because you are also a
Molder of men

I thought I was educated
I had read many books
But your knowledge of life revealed to me
How the world really looks

Teacher, you helped me to
Curtail my drinking
Which had gone out of control
I was going down real fast
Your love lifted me up and
Made my inhibitions unfold

You even taught me
The telephone can really
Open the line of communication
I had considered having it removed
Now, you can call me anytime
Because you have a reserved invitation

You lectured me on my confidence
A discipline I had forgotten
You even told me how to
Budget my money
By buying the best bargain

You schooled me on
Who were my true friends
And not to take myself for granted
Now I give myself top priority
I give you credit
For making the difference

Darling, I call you teacher
Not because you have a
B.S., M.A., or a P.H.D.
I address you as teacher
Because you understand me better than
I know me

Teacher, you reprimanded me
Because I was asking an "A" in the streets
And a "D" at home
Now you have my love
Because you showed me
Together we belong

I love you teacher

Technological Survival

So they can make gasohol from plants
They've already gone to the moon
They even have modular housing
With robots to take over soon

You can go around the world
Before daylight turns to night
Then go home to bed
At the end of your flight

Yet people are starving
The numbers increase everyday
And people are consistently
Blowing each other away

There is no end to this injustice to
Human beings
Why not peace, love and happiness
That notion was crushed
When they dethroned our King

Why can't we live as one people
In this life
This mandate should last forever
The thought sure is nice

Let's start now
There is no time to wait
Technological survival
Will determine our fate

The Fall Of Alexander Haig

A Westpoint graduate
Decorated soldier of fortune
To this four-star general
Everyone was subordinate

He rose to top
Starting as a lieutenant
His ultimate goal
To become U.S. President

The fall of Alexander Haig
He came too far, too fast
The fall of Alexander Haig
Just like the Roman Class

This Secretary of the State
Was just a heartbeat away
From being Commander-and-Chief
Haig would not take orders
He was always very brief

"I'm in charge"
The Falklands insurrection
A fired U.N. Ambassador
Led to his irrevocable termination

The fall of Alexander Haig
Once a powerful military leader
The fall of Alexander Haig
Wisely defeated

The Human Side

He always looks angry
She never smiles
They both act tough
From the other side of town

We are all uniquely different
Peculiarly—we are the same
We all have a destiny
In life's enigmatic game

No matter how adverse you are
Your human side will shine through
Most of us have a sense of decency
The human side is proof

You may be down to no good
At home there may be a
Husband, wife or kids
You will shield them from trouble
Because you are involved with it

With your double-dealing
There is a strong possibility
You will be caught
That is when you realize
Life is only a bout

Inside your head
A solution is contained
The human side is real
Your heart frames
The human side you feel

The Hurt I've Seen (Is The Pain I Feel)

The hurt I've seen (is the pain I feel)
The hurt I've seen (won't it heal)

My eyes have participated in
Life's trying events
They have been traumatized
All but spent

Early on it started
Even before adolescence
Include disenchantment
If I reminisce

The hurt I feel (is the pain I feel)
Happiness I am without
The hurt I feel (is the pain I feel)
Resentment is about

It is an individual situation
Multiplied by many
Too many stories contained
Within this entity

Hiding is inconceivable
My emotions are imprisoned internally
There are an abundance-
Of the world—I am lonely

The hurt I've seen (is the pain I feel)
A bitter taste twists my mouth
The hurt I've seen (is the pain I feel)
Positions it with doubt

The Innerwoman

She comes on rough and tough
Inside she is mellow
She talks strong and blunt
That is not her endeavor

She wants you to think
She is cruel
Although she is at peace

It appears, for a man
She has no need
When he is her relief

Men, before you become offended
Recognize the innerwoman
She may like you a lot
The innerwoman

Her motives may seem selfish
She has disguised her reasons long
Competition she welcomes
She yearns to hear your song

At times she pretends
To be domineering and
Conceal her sensitive feelings
Your manhood she suppresses
She doesn't want her heart revealing

The innerwoman is really
Soft as cotton
The innerwoman
Has never forgotten

Myles W. Wallace

The Lady With The White Pants

She was poured in her pants
They fit like a glove
Tight around the hips
They hugged every curve

She wore under alls beneath
There were no lines
Include the fact
The lady was fine

She was jet black
A stallion if there ever was
When she walked
My heart spoke—love

I called her white pants
Skin of cream
White pants was
A living dream

Her derriere was perfect
So was the rest
And on top of that
The lady had common sense

She didn't have an attitude
She was a star
To me she was
Way above par

With her
You didn't need a spare
She was sweet and
Always had the upper hand

The lady with the white pants
Was a pretty baby
White pants was
A heck of a lady

The Man With The Golden Tip Finger

They laugh and giggle
Every where he touches
They squirm and wiggle
After him they rush

Their most sensuous points
He already knew
His roaming hands
Were always in hot pursuit

The man with the golden tip finger
Had the midas touch
The man with the golden tip finger
In them he had total trust

He penetrates their minds and
Infiltrates their hearts
He is straight as an arrow
He is always sharp

His tempting poise
Leaves no room for escape
Before you can react
He is at home plate

The man with the golden tip finger
His intensity is hot as a flame
The man with the golden tip finger
The ladies love his game

The More I Didn't Want To Be Him (The More I Look Like Him)

Growing up
I didn't want to be like Dad
Oh no! It wasn't something
He didn't have

When I look at the mirror
The more I act like him
In his reflection
Even more I am him

The more I didn't want to be him
The more I look like him
An inseparable trait

The more I didn't want to be him
The more I look like him
From him I was made

I always thought
He didn't understand life
Now I find myself
Using his advice

I will teach my children
All of his values
To keep their heads high and
Never look back

The more I didn't want to be him
The more I act like him
He is a winner

The more I didn't want to be him
The more I am him
Dad is my beginning

The Words You Say Now
(You Will Eventually Understand)

You fill her head full of fairy tales or
Something you saw on television
All the time you know
She possesses sincere inhibitions

Sweet nothings in her ear
Promises you cannot fulfill
Adventures in paradise and
Excursions to the top of the hill

The words you say now
(You will eventually understand)
Now, they have no meaning

The words you say now
(You will eventually understand)
Because, you have no feelings

You wine and dine her
Motivated by delusion of grandeur
You gave her a tiny ring
Which you classified extravagant

You are surviving just off
The edge of imagination
To her you make constant untrue statements
You are compelled by false determination

The words you say now
(You will eventually understand)
Your fate the future holds

The words you say now
(You will eventually understand)
For your tales told

"There Are Fires,"
The Sinking Of The H.M.S. Sheffield

From solid steel she was built
Designed to last
The pride of Britain's Royal Navy
This ship had class

Her top speed—forty knots
With armada and radar
She was almost indestructible
Some would say, too comfortable

Remember the Delgado,
The A-4 skyhawk's pilot said
As he took aim
From missile to target
Was twenty miles away

The warhead exploded
A direct shot
"Abandon ship!"
Captain "Sam" called out

"There are fires
We are sinking fast
There are fires
Flames everywhere"

Smoke poured through
A gaping hole in her side
Sailors waked
In her tide

Her engines revved
Trying to escape disaster
Her bow tilted
Taking water faster

Her fate was imminent
The final plunge
Captain "Sam" shouted
For heroes unsung

"There are fires
The metal is red hot
There are fires
And we can't put them out"

There Is Only One

Let's conserve
There is only one earth
Though we might not deserve

There is only one sky
This we cannot deny

There is only one moon
Though, always not in bloom

There is only one sun
Without it, there would be no fun

There is only one water
Let's keep it flowing

Air surrounds
Without it, no one would survive

There Ought To Be Law

The way you wiggle your hips
How you test and tease
Twist and sway
You keep me uneasy

You stick out
In just the right places
You leave men blushing
All over their faces

There ought to be a law
The new first amendment
There ought to be a law
For your shrewd intentions

You think
When others are sleeping
"Alice in Wonderland"
You're always pretending

You like mini-skirts
Above your knees
Go-go boots below

See through blouses
Opened to your belly button
Crammed in a tight leather coat

There ought to be a law
Sanctioned by the Supreme Court
There needs to be a law
With full legislative support

They Tell Us To Be Honest
(White Collar Crime)

Some call it embezzlement
When they rob us blind
Others call it cheating
It's still a crime

They tell us to be honest
That's white collar crime
They want us to be honest
They don't do any time

We can barely get welfare
Businesses receive plenty of help
Corporations get subsidies and
The worker hardly makes a cent

They tell us to be honest
That's white collar crime
They tell us to be honest
Brother can you spare a dime

This Rose Simply Says: I Love You

This rose simply says: I love you

You can wear it in your hair
To adorn your lovely face
Plant it in your garden
For love always

This rose simply says: I love you

Or put it in your hand
Let the wind blow its course
My rose will soar and
Spread love broad

This rose simply says: I love you

Those Darn Flies

Batting, flapping and swiping
He tries to wipe years away
His testimony to longevity
As he rocks and sways

The buzz him continuously
Especially his head and ears
Sometimes they stop
But they are always near

Those darn flies
The substance of time
Those darn flies
Once they were beside

The faster he swings
The more they strike
One hit right after another
There is no reliever
Or running for cover

The best he can do
Is go for a walk
During that time
They never halt

Those darn flies
They are forever present
The darn flies
For the final chapter

Triple T From Texas

His name is Thomas Tenotchie Tankersley
He lives on tenth street in Tyler, Texas
He is the twelfth child in his family
He has ten nieces and ten nephews
That live next door in a enormous trailer

His kin call him Bob
He didn't like the idea of
Relatives shortening his name and saying
"Hey Uncle Tom"

Triple T from Texas is
Tawny, tenacious, tight
Triple T from Texas is
Tough, truthful, taut

For a living
He drives a two-ton tow-truck
His wife's name is Tina
For fun, he likes to the theater
He does not own a tv

He takes his occupation seriously
Triple T will listen to you twice
He is a top-notch person
He does things right

Triple T from Texas is
Terrific, tireless, trying
Triple T from Texas is
Tops, tremendous, towering

Truth Is Strange As Fiction

My girl left
Yesterday she cared
Love vanished
Right—into thin air

Happy moments shared
Turned into pain
Vows we said are
Silent for hearts refrain

Truth is strange as fiction
Edgar Allen Poe
Truth is strange as fiction
Behind the steel door

The world we knew
Is now a different land
The future we discussed
Are another's plans

I wait for the phone to ring
As it always did
When I call her number
A recording says no one is in

Truth is strange as fiction
Like a science book
Truth is strange as fiction
Love I mistook

TV

Dialogue has deteriorated
Acting is outrageous
Dime store productions
Inflated wages

Plots are weak
Scripts are thin
You can tell
It is an act
From start to end

TV is all downhill
TV is terminally ill

Pompadour hairstyles
Imitation makeup
One minute news
Anchor breakup

Everyone is so fashion conscious
It is such a charade
You might as well be watching a
Dingle berry parade

The early days were better
Let's bring them back
People were real
The pictures were fact

TV is a total turnoff
TV should go off

Twerp

He minds others business
Always snooping around
He knows everything about anybody
Even those out of town

A true busy body
He keeps his eyes on everything
A sure hear-it-all
He might say anything

Twerp is synonymous with jerk
Twerp gets on your last nerve

His ears are like antennas
They hear like a cauliflower buds
Gossip is his agenda
Rumors are his urge

He could be a spy
So watch what you say on the telephone
Don't ever invite him
Into your home

Twerp, get out, go, scat
Twerp, now run and tell that

Using Me

We met, then you went away
I found another
Then you lost your lover
Now you want to come back to stay

I am happy with who I have
And there is no way
You can fit into my plans

You want to get back into my life
You even moved into the same building
You tell everyone you meet
How we were living

You're using me
Why don't you just go away
You're using me
Our romance was yesterday

I think you still care
But you had your chance
You chose not to
Put me in your permanent plans

You are trying to rekindle
A forgotten flame
The fire left long ago
Our situation will never be the same

Go back
To wherever you were
Just forget about me
I am too much in love

You're using me
For your own selfish desires
You're using me
You were never mine

We Look In Love

We make a lovely couple
You have a beautiful smile
We look so perfect
When we paint the town

It is just an illusion
At home it is a different story
It is dog eat dog
Nothing like our outside glory

We look in love
It is only a mirage
We look in love
A total facade

When we first married
I thought it would last forever
Vows we wanted to uphold
Just like our parents

We walk around
Like everything is lovy-duby
When in realty
We do not even like each other

We look in love
Just faking
We look in love
Hearts breaking

What Is Black?

Is it a fist pushed through the air
Is it an education
Perhaps it's braided hair
A unique combination

A certain manner of dress
Maybe it's the type of shoes
Is it partying the best
Or a particular type of food

What is black?
You tell me

What is black
Open your heart and see

Is it the way of the walk
Or where one lives
Is it the hep talk
Like the rap to win

The kind of car
The beverage drank
Maybe it is the thoughts of the mind
Pressure the brink

What is black?
It is nothing new

What is black
It's me, it's you

Myles W. Wallace

When The Glitter Is Gone

When the curtain is down
And your youth is done
To who will you turn
To hear your song

You say you will wait
Till the time comes
By then it will be too late
If you would slow down a minute
Just to think

When the glitter is gone
There will be no escape
When the glitter is gone
The way this game is played

Remember the times
You are fancy free
That is your way to live
Oh! So short! So brief!

Maturation will set in
You will miss the beat
Then you will realize
Your life is so incomplete

When the glitter is gone
The fountain will spring no more
When the glitter is gone
You will know the score

"Whenever I say America"

I say so many things!-

Something shouts in the syllables,
Something echoes and sings

Maybe it's hope,
Maybe it's pride,
Maybe it's only love

Maybe it's a kind of hail
To the flag that flies above

The flag flies so broad and bright
From dawn to setting sun

It takes the wind and takes
the light-
The flag our fathers won!

When I say "America"
Old pictures come to me
Of lone prowls
Pushing slowly across the sea

Of men and women who knew no
rest

Toiling with heart and hand;

Of covered wagons rocking west,

Into an unknown land;

Of freemen striving, striving
still

Myles W. Wallace

In freedom's old hard way . . .

Whenever I say "America"

So many things I say

-Shirlesha Rogers-
April 28, 1997

Whenever I Think Of Smart

My dad gave me a one dollar bill
Because I am his best son
I traded it to my buddy
For two dollars
Because two is more than one

Then I took the dollars and
Swapped them with another pal
For three five dollar bills
I did not tell him
Three is better still

Along came Mr. Bates
People say he can't see
He gave me four ten dollar bills
For my three five dollar bills
Four is definitely more than three

I took the ten dollar bills to Hiram
Down at the corner store
The man gave me five fifty dollar bills
Five is a lot more than four

Finally I went home and
Showed the money to my dad
He was so happy, he was so proud
He shook my hand

Then he asked me where
I got two-hundred-fifty dollars from
I told him I had done an act
He said "son that isn't fair
"Find those people and
"Give them their money back!"

I thought about what my father said
I said "dad you're right!"
I found Hiram and
Gave him his fifties back

I caught up with my buddy
After I had seen the rest
I returned his two dollars for my dollar
Now I feel alright, I feel great

The moral of my story is
You can make money being dishonest
Just remember, one thing
The best policy is to always be honest

By: Joshua Jones—April 28, 1997

Who Took Christ Out Of Christmas

The birthday of our Lord
Has been replaced with commercialism
The year of the Lord
Is paid television

We should celebrate Christmas
Precisely for what it represents
The salvation of humankind
By our Lord
Not by providing presents

Someone took Christ out of Christmas
And replaced him with money
Whoever took Christ out of Christmas
Omitted the man of wonders

It is better to give, than receive
Just do it for the Lord
He will forever guide your way
Sunny or storm

Let's put Christ back in Christmas
It is him, we need to respect
Christ is Christmas
Pagans we should always reject

Whoever took Christ out of Christmas
Forgot what Christmas is about
Whoever took Christ out of Christmas
Did not care that Christmas counts

Put Christ back in Christmas and
The meaning of Christmas
Will be resolved
Keep Christ in Christmas
To remain with the Lord on solid ground

Christmas is more than just a holiday
Christmas should be celebrated everyday
Put Christ back in Christmas and
Keep Christmas that way

Myles W. Wallace

Why Do They Make It So Hard

I went to the Doctor
I told him I had a stomach ache
He gave me a peculiar look and said
Sit down and wait

He told he had to run
A battery of tests
I just burped
What else with indigestion

After the investigation
He wanted me to take an E.K.G.
I asked him, was that
Something he had seen on N.B.C.

Then he checked my blood, temperature
Eyes, ears, nose and throat
Including everything else
He charged me two-hundred-fifty dollars and
Put the check in his chest

He wrote a prescription
On extremely thin paper
The message was so light
You could not cut it with a razor

Finally, after all of
This diagnostic misbehavior
The note read
"Take two aspirin with flavor
Get some rest
And have a nice day!"
Yeah.

Why You Brother

You were sitting on top
A fuel laden rocket
Strapped in the shuttle—Challenger
Pointed to out-of-space

Down here—on earth
This is your place
It is your home
For goodness sakes!

I was watching television
I could not believe that it was true
Tears shut my eyes
I just couldn't get you out my mind
Your face filled my view

One and one/half minutes after lift-off
There was a tremendous explosion
Now you are in the clouds
My heart is overcome with emotion

There's was no possible escape
Oh my God! I shuddered
I said to myself
Why you brother

Doing your duty
You knew the risks involved
The man that you were
I salute you—proud

You were a star athlete
Who made football a winning scheme
A saxophonist whose instrument
Produced music so sweet
A champion of the people
For the world to see

Tributes, praises and honorable words
Continue to be said
But, I just can't
Get you out of my head
Why? Why you brother and
I don't know if I ever will recover

There are reasons for everything
That happen in life
Some—humans will never understand
I just can't believe
This was journey's end

They can put the blame on overworked workers
A failure in the rocket booster
A flaw in the o-ring's design
Cold weather or failed sensors
Or it was your time

They can say anything they want
It's just old news
Ronald McNair, age 35
Married father of two

I know you never suffered
The question that goes unanswered is
Why you brother?

Wild In The Country

I'm not talking about hayrides
Or marshmallow roasts
Hotdogs, chopping wood and
Drinking cokes

It's time to party
A festival of sorts
I am inviting everyone
To see how far we can go

Wild in the country
To the top of the world
Buck wild in the country
Jump on for a whirl

Ladies, ladies, ladies
Yeah, wine, women and song
This is more than a get-to-together
We are going to have
One heck of a ball

We are going to party
Until there's no end in sight
We're really going to get down
Until dawn turns to night

Wild in the country
Let's whip it up
Hog wild in the country
Ye ha!

Yes You Are

You are my baby
Oh yes you are
Yes you are

You are my baby
Oh yes you are

You are baby
Whether near or far
Yes you are
You are, you are

You are my lady
Oh yes you are
Yes you are

You are my lady
Yes you are
You are, you are

You are my light
You are, you are
Oh yes, yes you are

You are my day
You are, you are
You are

You are my sun
You are, you are
You are

You are my baby
You are, you are
Oh yes you are
Yes you are
Oh yes you are

You Are My Standard

Your smile is live
Your personality shows it
Your style is wonderful
Your conscious sees fit

Your friends are nice people
Your interests—neat
Even the earth you walk on
Appreciates your feet

You are my standard
My measure of life
You are my standard
You always do right

You ask for nothing
You find ways to give
I will follow your example
That is how I want to live

People you meet
Treat you like family
Total strangers
Talk to you friendly

You are my standard
Your heart is gold
You are my standard
On you, I am sold

Myles W. Wallace

You Make Me Hard

I become like superman's fist
When I see you
More rigid than an erector set
When you are near me too

I feel like a diamond
For cutting plate glass
Just like an oak
On fertile land

You make me hard
Stronger than steel
You keep me hard
With an iron will

I'm like hickory
For making chairs
Just like a flagpole
Tall I stand

Like the wood of
A bowling pin
I don't stay down long
Before I'm up again

You make me hard
Hard as
A roll of half-dollars

Baby, you keep me hard
Harder than
A government audit

You Say One Thing/But Mean Another

You talk about loving me
When you are already with someone
When I call you
There is no response

You say you will be with me
In time of need
My only companion is
Constant misery

You say one thing/but mean another
Just talking out both sides of your mouth
You say one thing/but mean another
You have no idea what you are talking about

You tell friends
We are real tight
But I never have the chance
To kiss you goodnight

You want everything
To be just one way and
Keep me wrapped up
While you play

You say one thing/but mean another
You want to have your cake and eat it too
You say one thing/but mean another
Your world was made only for you

You Will Always Be That Beautiful To Me

When you were first born
People said you were a cute baby and
They would give the world
Plus everything else you wanted
They based their feelings on
Your anticipated adult behavior

You are a grown woman now
They still tell you, you're pretty, even fine
You have a destination in life
Working is something you always did
Because you always found the time

You are very attractive
This I admit
You have got nice legs
A small waistline and most of all
You have common sense

With your cute smile
And dimpled nose
A perfect set of lips and
A model's measurements
You strike a picture post card pose

Several men have offered to take care of you
They even wanted to buy you diamonds and furs
They would kiss the ground on which you walk
While catering to your every wish
They tell you they are in love

You will always be that beautiful to me
Even in one-hundred years
You will always be that beautiful to me
Your beauty is perfectly clear

You head is placed high in the air
You are tactful—but direct to the point
If a person doesn't says something you don't like
You turn your back
Instead of telling them to get lost

You will always be that beautiful to me
Tempting temptation
You will always be that beautiful to me
I am totally infatuated

You don't use your looks
Which are in the eyes of the beholders
To think you are prima donna
You don't want to live high
Nor do want to try to get over

Somewhere in the future
Perhaps we can come together
Before mother nature makes her choice
And father time does the same
While brother murphy speaks his voice

You will always be that beautiful to me
Your face should be a million dollar bill
You will always be that beautiful to me
Supremely beautiful, if you will

Your Complexion

Your complexion is beautiful
Skin of bronze
Made in heaven
High above

Your skin is a mixture of
Silk and honey
In this world, to me
You mean more than money

You shine like a light
From the brilliant sky
Radiating beauty
Loveliness that will
Never be denied

Baby, keep on glowing
Sweetheart, you are what
Keeps life going

Your Love Brings Out The Best In Me

With you I am always happy
I am never sad
You keep me smiling
I am so glad

I walk with pride
On top of the world
I constantly boast
You are my girl

Your love brings out the best in me
You earned an "A"
Your love brings out the best in me
With a gold star behind your name

I treat my friends
With more respect
It is not in my heart
People to reject

Work is great
School is a thrill
I am king of the mountain
I don't worry about bills

Your love brings out the best in me
Thank you, baby
Your love brings out the best in me
I love your way

Your Picture Is Worth (1000 Words)

I look at your photo
And smile
I haven't heard from you
In a while

If the telephone doesn't ring
You are always close
When my door doesn't open
I want you most

Your picture is worth (1000 words)
With it near
Your picture is worth (1000 words)
I have you here

You left for a journey
To become in touch with life
In my heart
I know you're right

One day you will return
Until then, I will remain composed
In the mean time
Your photograph shows

Your picture is worth (1000 words)
It is all I need
Your picture is worth (1000 words)
To keep me company

Your Way

You see them in three-piece suits
Walking like tin soldiers
Ages 25-50
They never grow older

They look like choir boys
With angel faces
Acting like the pillsbury dough boy
With inner tubes around their waists

Do it your way
Just be yourself

Do it your way
Improve what you do best

They speak the Kings English
No word can they spell
When you turn your back
They tell you: "Go to Hell!"

They have three martini lunches
Wives they never see
They are too busy pretending
Something they will never be

Do it your way
Games you don't have to play

Do it your way
You won't have to fake

You've Got To Love Somebody

You think you've got it made, yet
You come home all to yourself
You're in love with material possessions
You've placed your heart on a shelf

You can go out and buy
Anything that you want
There's no price tag on love
But your mind tells you don't

You've got to love somebody
You have to hold and squeeze someone
You've got to love somebody
Or life is no fun

You can go to fancy restaurants
And other stylish places
Inside you hurt because all you see
Are smiling faces

You try to get away from it all
There is no running away
You need that special person
Just to make your day

You've got to love somebody
Don't put it off until tomorrow
You've got to love somebody
Without love, there is only sorrow